# SCIENCE AS INQUIRY
## IN THE SECONDARY SETTING

# SCIENCE AS INQUIRY
## IN THE SECONDARY SETTING

*Edited by Julie Luft, Randy L. Bell, and Julie Gess–Newsome*

**NSTA** press
National Science Teachers Association

Arlington, Virginia

National Science Teachers Association

Claire Reinburg, Director
Judy Cusick, Senior Editor
Andrew Cocke, Associate Editor
Betty Smith, Associate Editor
Robin Allan, Book Acquisitions Manager

**Art and Design**
Will Thomas, Jr., Director
Tim French, Senior Graphic Designer (cover and interior design)

**Printing and Production**
Catherine Lorrain, Director

**National Science Teachers Association**
Gerald F. Wheeler, Executive Director
David Beacom, Publisher

**Library of Congress Cataloging-in-Publication Data**
Science as inquiry in the secondary setting / edited by Julie Luft, Randy L. Bell, and Julie Gess-Newsome.
    p. cm.
 Includes bibliographical references and index.
 ISBN 978-1-933531-26-7
 1. Science--Study and teaching (Secondary)--United States.  2. Inquiry-based learning.  I. Luft, Julie.  II. Bell,
Randy L.  III. Gess-Newsome, Julie.
Q183.3.A1S3526 2007
507.1'2--dc22

                    2007042206

This book was made possible by National Science Foundation grant #0540041. The ideas expressed herein are those of the authors and do not reflect the views of personnel affiliated with the National Science Foundation.

# Contents

# Foreword

Science as inquiry has been at the forefront of science education reform since the mid-1990s. Curricular standards, instructional materials, and authentic assessments, coupled with the National Science Teachers Association's continuous support for inquiry-based science, have significantly raised the profile of science-as-inquiry in secondary school classrooms.

Even today, however, the phrase *science as inquiry* continues to conjure up multiple meanings and images of practice. Although the science education community recognizes inquiry as a centerpiece of science teaching and learning, many teachers are still striving to build a shared understanding of what science as inquiry means, and at the more practical level, what it looks like in the classroom.

In the NSF Foundations series monograph (2000), *Inquiry: Thoughts, Views, and Strategies for the K–5 Classroom,* experts in the field of elementary inquiry science shared their insights and experiences about inquiry-based science in the early, formative years. This monograph became a widely used resource to help elementary science educators introduce, implement, and sustain inquiry content and practices in their K–5 schools, classrooms, and preservice programs.

Now, with *Science as Inquiry in the Secondary Setting*, we have a full picture of K–12 inquiry. *Science as Inquiry in the Secondary Setting* moves beyond "inquiry science rhetoric" and connects school science to authentic characteristics of the scientific community. Addressing the critical importance of a high-quality secondary science education, this book brings inquiry-based teaching and learning together in a conceptually and strategically powerful way. The authors are not just armchair theorists. Their work and research are grounded in teachers' classrooms, and the rich vignettes and examples they include help the reader make connections between the information presented and what it looks like in practice.

Whether you have already begun your journey into teaching science through inquiry or are just starting, you will find this book to be a welcome catalyst for your professional growth. Although individuals can gain considerable new knowledge by reading this book on their own, powerful new learning will result when the book's chapters are shared through discussion with fellow science educators at all levels, including preservice teachers, inservice teachers, and those who educate teachers of science. Professional learning communities will find this book to be an excellent resource to provoke thinking and stimulate conversation in collaborative settings. Reading chapters at regular intervals and coming together as a learning community to discuss implications for improved teaching and learning can stretch teachers in thinking beyond their current practice, stimulate growth and renewal, and help jump-start future and new teachers in the early stages of their careers.

By moving away from the isolation of individual classrooms toward supporting science classrooms in which all students in a middle or high school are actively engaged in authentic science learning, teachers will see measurable scores of skills and knowledge increase. Just as important, they will see their students' deeper engagement with, interest in, and appreciation of science grow and flourish.

Get ready for an intellectually inspiring and challenging experience as your journey into inquiry either begins or continues with this book. Whatever your level of teaching experience and wherever you or your professional learning community chooses to start in this book, each chapter will challenge you to think about your own beliefs about learning, teaching practice, and students in new ways—ways that will ultimately help all students to succeed in school and in life.

—Page Keeley
NSTA President-Elect 2007–08
Science Program Director,
Maine Mathematics and Science Alliance

# Preface

Science as Inquiry in the Secondary Setting and its companion volumes, *Technology in the Secondary Science Classroom* (now available from the National Science Teachers Association [NSTA]) and *Science Education Reform in the Secondary Setting* (in development at NSTA), have a long and interesting history. The ideas for these books emerged from our work with secondary science teachers, supportive program officers at the National Science Foundation, and the science education community, which is always seeking a connection of theory and practice. In order to ensure that these books were connected to each of these stakeholders, we adopted a writing plan that involved representatives from all three groups. We considered novel approaches to identify and support science teachers and science educators to participate in the project, and we sought guidance from program officers about the format and dissemination of the final product.

To begin with, we identified three topics of interest to both science teachers and science educators—science as inquiry, educational technology, and science education reform. We wanted the community of science educators to help define the content of each book, so we solicited chapter proposals from science teachers and science educators. The response was impressive, with over 50 chapter proposals submitted for the three books. Our selection of the chapters was based on the clarity of the topic, the type of idea presented, and the importance of the topic to science teachers.

Chapter authors were then asked to generate a first draft. These chapters were shared among the authors of their respective books for review. We met as a group at the annual meeting of the Association of Science Teacher Educators, in Portland, Oregon, to discuss and provide feedback to one another on our chapters. This session was extremely useful, and several of the authors returned to their chapters, ready for another revision.

Once the second revision was complete, we wanted to draw on the expertise of science teachers, whom we felt should ground this work. We contacted NSTA and placed a "call for reviewers" in their weekly electronic newsletter. Over 200 teachers offered to review our chapters. Reviews were shared with the chapter authors.

The second revision was also shared among the authors within each book. Each author now had external reviews from teachers, as well as reviews from other authors. To discuss these reviews and the final revision of the chapters, we met one more time at the annual meeting of the National Association for Research in Science Teaching, in San Francisco, California. At the conclusion of this meeting, chapter authors were ready to write their final versions.

When the chapters were completed and the books were in a publishable format, we approached NSTA about publishing them both in print and online, so that they would reach as many teachers as possible. NSTA has historically offered one chapter of a book for free, but the opportunity to break new ground by offering each chapter of this book free online would be new publishing territory. Of course, paper copies of each book are available for purchase, for those who prefer print versions. We also asked, and NSTA agreed, that any royalties from the books would go to NSTA's teacher scholarship fund to enable teachers to attend NSTA conferences.

This process has indeed been interesting, and we would like to formally thank the people who have been helpful in the development and dissemination of these books. We thank Carole Stearns for believing in this project; Mike Haney for his ongoing support; Patricia Morrell for helping to arrange meeting rooms for our chapter reviews; the 100+ teachers who wrote reviews on the chapters; Claire Reinburg, Judy Cusick, and Andrew Cocke of NSTA for their work on these books; Lynn Bell for her technical edits of all three books; and the staff at NSTA for agreeing to pilot this book in a downloadable format so it is free to any science teacher.

—Julie Luft, Randy L. Bell, and Julie Gess-Newsome

# What Is Inquiry? A Framework for Thinking About Authentic Scientific Practice in the Classroom

**I**

Mark Windschitl, University of Washington

The idea of inquiry can be perplexing to many of us in science education. The National Science Education Standards (NRC 1996, p. 31) proclaim that inquiry is "at the heart of science and science learning" and represents "the central strategy for teaching science." Yet, if you were to visit a number of typical classrooms where students were purportedly engaged in inquiry, you would likely have great difficulty figuring out what the various activities had in common.

In one high school for example, a group of 10th-grade biology students might be trying to determine the source of pollution in a local stream and how they could clean it up. Just down the hall, a group of 12th graders in a physics class might be conducting student-designed investigations on the thermal insulating properties of manufactured materials. Across the street at the junior high school, 8th-grade Earth science students might be following a highly structured protocol to find the densities of mineral samples, while the 7th graders next door might be writing a research paper on how climate change influenced the extinction of the woolly mammoth.

Teachers in each of these classrooms would likely refer to their instruction as inquiry based, and each of these scenarios could indeed be broadly described as "working out answers to questions or problems." But these examples are not simply variations on a theme—the intellectual work required of students and the learning outcomes in each of these cases are fundamentally different.

In this chapter, a framework is suggested for organizing teacher thinking about inquiry and prioritizing the wide assortment of activities teachers typically use to familiarize their students with the processes of science. This framework articulates three families of school science activity. One family represents the core knowledge-building practices of science. A second represents activities that support the core practices in various ways. And a third family of activities—common practices that need to be reconsidered—actually distracts students from meaningful learning.

# Family 1: The Core Knowledge-Building Activities of Science

Scientists engage in a wide range of activities. They watch other members of their profession perform demonstrations of new equipment and techniques, they build laboratory skills over time (e.g., safety practices, using equipment, learning specific procedures), they replicate other scientists' experiments, they invent new technologies, they conduct thought experiments, they conduct library research, and they use knowledge to solve practical problems. All of these activities are valuable for school science learning as well, but there are particular practices that are integral to the core work of science—this core being organized around the development of defensible explanations of the way the natural world works (see, e.g., Giere 1991; Longino 1990). Roughly speaking, these explanations come from the process of developing models and hypotheses and then testing them against evidence derived from observation and experiment.

## Four Conversations That Make Up the Core Knowledge-Building Activities

When we think of doing science, we usually envision a laboratory or field activity—for example, people working with materials, collecting data, graphing results—but these activities are only part of the story. Scientists are ultimately engaged in developing persuasive arguments around competing explanations for natural occurrences. Everything else that comes before (the questioning, the hypothesizing, the measuring, the analyzing) merely sets the groundwork for the culminating argument. So, although the investigative *activity* provides the critical context for learning, the *science-specific forms of talk* move scientists' (or students') thinking forward.

Think of this talk as a set of four interrelated conversations that support students' understanding of the intellectual and material work of science.

1. Organizing what we know and what we'd like to know.

2. Generating a model.

3. Seeking evidence.

4. Constructing an argument.

As students are invited to participate in these conversations, they come to understand that "science talk" is a system of rhetoric with certain conventions about the topics of conversation (what happens in the natural world), forms of knowledge used (theories, models, laws, facts), rules for argument (e.g., explanations must be coherent, plausible, and consistent with evidence), and goals (producing explanatory accounts for natural phenomena).

Before these four conversations begin, the teacher must set the stage by considering some puzzling or otherwise motivating problem with which students can engage. Not all interesting ideas are equally important; those that can be used to explain other phenomena in the world are more central to science than are ideas that are interesting but do not increase our understanding of the world.

Studying widely applicable ideas like wave motion, inheritance, or chemical equilibrium, for example, provides students with powerful conceptual tools for understanding much of what they see around them. By comparison, if your students are interested in the relative absorbency of different brands of paper towels or finding which glue has the strongest adhesive properties, the knowledge they gain will not likely be useful in other circumstances. The point here is that inquiry experiences should foster a deep and well-integrated understanding of important content, as well as the reasoning skills and practices of science—the separation of "learning content" and "doing inquiry" is entirely unnecessary. Once interest is established in a motivating and conceptually important topic, the first of the four conversations can begin.

*Conversation 1: Organizing What We Know and What We'd Like to Know.*
In school science, students often begin investigations with surprisingly sparse and disorganized background knowledge, which leads to superficial inquiries that add only trivial descriptive notes to what they know and fails to explore underlying causes for phenomena. Students must first gather background information on the inquiry topic (e.g., from hands-on activities, texts, guest speakers, the media, or the internet or by making systematic observations of the phenomena in question). They should then organize and "externalize" their thinking on paper in the form of scientific models.

Scientific models represent ideas—ideas of how the natural world is structured or how it operates. Models can take many forms in science (e.g., written explanations, concept maps, graphs, diagrams, equations, physical representations). Regardless of the forms they take, models are anchored in phenomena and represent interrelationships among entities, properties, events, and processes. Some models are subsets of larger systems of explanation referred to as "theory" (e.g., theories of evolution, plate tectonics, molecular motion), and others represent everyday events such as the feeding habits of fish in an aquarium or the means by which a bike helmet protects a cyclist's head in an accident.

As an example, a group of 9th graders were curious about why objects feel as if they weigh less under water. Their teacher wanted to see which conceptual frameworks the students used to think about this problem and asked them to draw a diagram of how they thought forces acted on a submerged mass. The students' initial model, however, failed to suggest why the mass weighed less after it was submerged (A in Figure 1.1). B in Figure 1.1 is a more accurate version that was developed after some instruction, and C and D in Figure 1.1 are even more developed models that could be used to explain a variety of phenomena, including why submarines risk having their hulls crushed at great depths. Developing such representations is important to the learning process because

- they can be shared with others and critiqued;

- they can help learners see connections between ideas in ways that other representations (such as oral explanations) will not allow;

- they can be changed as the class (or individual) learns more; and

- the production of models helps teachers recognize gaps in students' thinking that must be addressed before the inquiry can move forward.

Students should learn to talk about the framework of their existing knowledge *as* a model—recognizing that models are not "copies of reality," that a model is tentative and can contain unseen entities or processes (such as forces and buoyancy in Figure 1.1), that there can be multiple forms of models for the same phenomenon, and that models help generate ideas.

FIGURE 1.1. PROGRESSIVE MODELS OF FORCE ON A SUBMERGED OBJECT

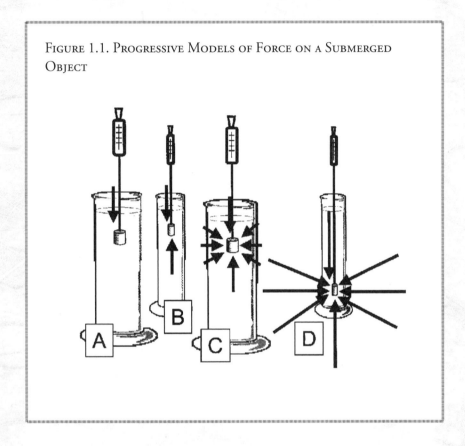

Based on the idea that "organizing what we know and what we'd like to know" is a critical first step in authentic inquiry, certain kinds of student conversations are necessary to make this a meaningful process within the larger context of the investigation. The following are a number of key questions that engage students in such conversations (not all can be explored, of course, in any one inquiry).

- What do we already know about this situation, process, or event?

- Could there be more than one way to represent this situation, event, or process?

- Is our model purely descriptive of the situation, process, or event, or does it have parts that try to explain what is happening?

- What questions does this model help us ask?

- What additional information do we need in order to improve the initial model before asking our final inquiry questions?

- How can our questions be framed so that they can be answered by collecting and analyzing data?

*Conversation 2: Generating a Model.* Models created by students represent their best current understanding of how some aspect of the world works. Students' inquiry questions should relate to some puzzling "piece" of this model. The model not only helps prompt more informed questions, it becomes the logical basis of the hypothesis. A hypothesis is a prediction for the kind of results one would expect from data collection if the initial model were accurate or complete. For example, students might use the model in C in Figure 1.1 to predict that a mass weighs less when immersed just below the surface, and this weight does not change significantly when it is submerged at greater depths.

As mentioned earlier, students may be so unfamiliar with a phenomenon that they will need to do some hands-on activity and make initial observations before they are able to develop any sort of model. Questions that can prompt students to explore a model include the following:

- Do we need to do some initial exploration and data collection before we can begin to develop a tentative model?

- What aspect of the model do we want to test?

- When we look at our tentative model and consider the question we want to ask, what would our model predict?

- How can we test the model in a way that generates better descriptions of how this phenomenon happens?

- Can we test the model in a way that helps us understand some process that is not directly observable?

These questions are often addressed in conjunction with the third set of conversations—referred to as seeking evidence.

***Conversation 3: Seeking Evidence.*** At this point, students have proposed a model and are considering what the model might predict about real-world outcomes. These outcomes are the products of systematic data collection. Data can be generated from controlled experiments, but data can also come from observations in which students do not actively manipulate variables (astronomers, for example, make carefully timed observations of new stars, and field biologists record the advance of invasive species in selected environments). Conversations about generating data should include the method students will use to analyze that data and represent it. Here are some questions that students need to discuss in order to grasp the meaning of "generating evidence" and be able to design their own studies eventually:

- How can we define our variables in ways that will allow us to record consistent and accurate measurements?

- How does the data we want to collect help us test our hypothesis?

- What will it mean to collect data "systematically"?

- To test our hypothesis, should we observe the world as it is or actively manipulate some variables while controlling others?

- When we analyze our data, will we compare groups? look for correlations between variables? seek other kinds of patterns?

- What forms of representation (e.g., tables, graphs, charts, diagrams) are most appropriate for the type of data we will collect?

***Conversation 4: Constructing an Argument.*** In science, arguments are about whether hypotheses, based on a model, "fit the world"—that is, are the data consistent with what the model predicted? Data become evidence when they are used to support an argument. The most famous investigations in science history had to be put forward to the science community as evidence-based arguments (the Sun-centered universe by Copernicus and Galileo, plate tectonics by Wegner, relativity by Einstein, natural selection by Darwin). Argument is not the same as stating a conclusion. Too often, students end their investigations by declaring that they found an unexpected trend, a difference between an experimental and control group, or some other pattern. They further claim that their data collection strategy was appropriate, that they were careful and accurate in collecting the data, and that they analyzed the data properly. Although these are important pieces of an argument, this way of ending an investigation neglects key elements of the persuasive core of science.

An authentic argument has four features:

1. It describes a potential explanation for the phenomenon of interest.

2. It uses the data collected as evidence to support this explanation.

3. It acknowledges any other possible explanations that would fit the data.

4. It describes if and how the initial model of the phenomenon should change in light of the evidence.

The following are questions students should explore as part of these conversations:

- Was the prediction of our original model consistent with the data we collected?

- Are we using our data to argue for a simple cause-and-effect relationship between variables, or are these variables only correlated (without causing one another)?

- Do the data provide support for theoretical (unobservable) processes in our model?

- How consistent and coherent is our final explanation for the phenomenon of interest?

- Do other possible explanations for the data exist, and if so, how strong is the evidence for these alternatives?

- Should our model change in light of the evidence?

## Summary of the Four Conversations

At first glance, it appears that these four sets of conversations should take place in the sequence described here, but they rarely do (see Figure 1.2). As with authentic inquiry conducted by scientists, student investigations are organic, recursive processes requiring students to revisit previous conversations constantly when new information emerges. For example, in the midst of data collection, even before it is analyzed, scientists often learn things that put them back into conversations about the models they had developed earlier. Revisiting previous conversations like this is the rule rather than the exception. Of course, no teacher can ask all of these questions during the course of any one inquiry, but every inquiry should include some parts of these four conversations. As students gain experience with guided forms of investigation, they become more competent inquirers by "internalizing" these conversations—eventually asking themselves these questions without prompting from the teacher. In this way they come to understand the meaning and interconnectedness of these scientific activities.

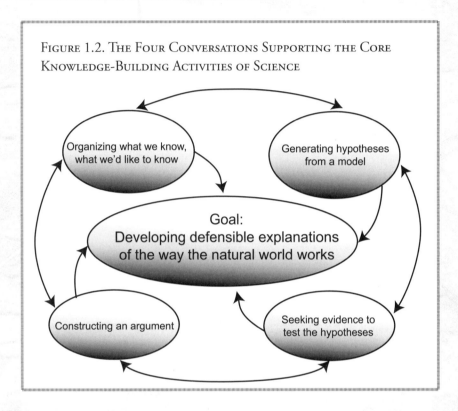

FIGURE 1.2. THE FOUR CONVERSATIONS SUPPORTING THE CORE KNOWLEDGE-BUILDING ACTIVITIES OF SCIENCE

A number of research reports provide evidence that this teaching approach is effective for learning both content and scientific reasoning. See, for example, research on high school students studying genetics (Cartier 2000) and physics topics (Wells, Hestenes, and Swackhamer 1995), middle school students inquiring about force and motion (Schwarz and White 2005), and 4th graders exploring how light interacts with materials (Magnussen and Palincsar 2005).

Two vignettes are included in this chapter that illustrate how teachers can infuse these critical conversations into an inquiry. The first is of an 8th-grade Earth science teacher using a guided investigation to help his students understand the relative motions of the Earth, Moon, and Sun. This example illustrates a number of opportunities for student talk and also demonstrates that inquiry can be used to deepen students' understanding of important concepts in science. This vignette is paraphrased from *Inquiry and the National Science Education Standards* (NRC 2000). The second vignette is based on the experiences of a 10th-grade biology teacher who had her students investigate the local causes of asthma in young people. It represents inquiry that emerges from student interest and is complex in that it has no single right answer.

## Vignette 1. Phases of the Moon[1]

Mr. Gilbert, a middle school teacher, knows that most of his students have difficulty constructing an explanation for the Moon's phases that is consistent with their everyday observations. He also knows that a grasp of this phenomenon is important because it demonstrates that objects in the solar system have predictable motion and that these motions explain other occurrences, such as eclipses, the year, and the day/night cycle.

Mr. Gilbert begins by asking his students what they think they know about the Moon and listing these ideas on the board (starting the "Organizing What We Know" conversation). The students call out that "the Moon changes shape," "the Moon is smaller than the Earth," and "people have walked on the Moon." Next Mr. Gilbert asks about questions they have and writes these out as well: "Should we try to land on the Moon again?" "Why don't eclipses happen more often?" "How wide across is the Moon?" and "How often do we get a full Moon?"

Mr. Gilbert realizes at this point that his students need more information before they can develop even a beginning model of the behavior of the Moon. Using homemade sextants constructed of protractors, straws, and string, he asks students to collect data about the position of the Moon in the sky and the Moon's shape. He then initiates a conversation around how to be systematic about collecting and recording this data (a part of the "Seeking Evidence" conversation). Some of his students comment that the Moon should be viewed at the same time every day. Others add that everyone should follow the same directions for using the sextants (see Sidebar 1).

A few weeks later, when students have made their observations, Mr. Gilbert returns to the Moon unit and asks students to display their observation charts on the wall of the classroom. Students talk about the patterns they see in the changing shape of the Moon and offer explanations that might account for their data. Prompted by these descriptive models, some students want to know what causes the patterns they have just witnessed. Mr. Gilbert presses everyone to suggest an explanatory account of the observed phenomenon (see Sidebar 2).

Some students immediately propose that the Earth's shadow covers different amounts of the Moon's surface at various times of the month. Others contend that as the Moon moves through its orbit we see different sides of the Moon illuminated by the Sun. Mr. Gilbert then asks students to divide into small groups and make a labeled drawing that supports each group's explanation for the Moon's changing shape (getting further into the "Organizing What We Know" conversation). He asks students to talk with one another about how they might use the models to test the two different explanations (starting the "Generating a Model" conversation).

The next day, students design an investigation using globes for the Earth, tennis balls for the Moon, and an overhead projector for the Sun (they participate in the second round of the "Seeking Evidence" conversation). Mr. Gilbert circulates among the groups, probing their understandings and focusing their thinking on the relationship between evidence and explanation: "Where would the Moon have to be in your model to result in a Quarter Moon?" "Show me where the Earth's shadow would be." "What evidence do you have that supports your conclusions or causes you to change your mind?" (See Sidebar 3.)

When needed, he asks students to refer back to their chart of the Moon's phases and reminds them, "A good model will explain that data" (all questions and prompts here are part of the "Constructing an Argument" conversation).

Mr. Gilbert begins the next class by asking each group to post its model drawings and invites the rest of the class to examine

## Sidebar 1

Here Mr. Gilbert has accomplished several things. First, the activity has generated interest and focused students on the phases of the Moon. Second, he has asked students to talk about what they currently understand about the Moon. This gives him a picture of what additional kinds of activity will be necessary for them to ask more meaningful questions. Third, the Moon-charting activity has allowed students to talk about being systematic in collecting data. The chart serves as a kind of initial model from which hypotheses can be generated.

## Sidebar 2

Mr. Gilbert now helps his students explore the difference between description and explanation. The students begin to offer hypotheses about what causes the Moon's phases, but Mr. Gilbert wants them to create explicit representations of how they think this phenomenon happens, prompting them to develop both a causal model and a hypothesis that can be logically derived from it.

## Sidebar 3

Here Mr. Gilbert repeatedly encourages students to talk about the relationship between their models, their hypotheses, and the evidence they are collecting.

the results. Most observations seem to support the explanation that as the Moon moves in orbit around the Earth the amount of the lighted side that can be seen from the Earth changes. The students agree that comparing the order of the phases in their model to the order of Moon phases shown on a calendar helps them assess the apparent relationship between the Earth, Sun, and Moon.

One team points out that during the first quarter phase of the Moon the Earth's shadow would have to turn at a right angle in order to fall on the Moon, and they note that light and shadows do not work that way (Figure 1.3).

FIGURE 1.3. STUDENT'S MODEL OF THE CAUSE OF MOON PHASES

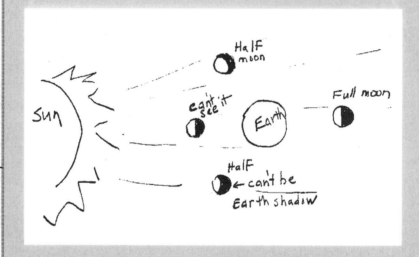

## Sidebar 4

In the final days of class, students are asked to share their models and reflect on and talk about how logical their model-based explanations are ("light cannot turn at right angles"), how predictive their models are, which features of their models work well and which don't, and how they might revise their models based on evidence and more library research.

Based on such evidence, even the students who proposed the "Earth's shadow" model decide to reject it. Mr. Gilbert adds a provocative question: "Some of your models predict that an eclipse would happen every month, but we know that doesn't happen. (See Sidebar 4.) How would we have to change your models so that doesn't happen?" He later asks, "Which features of your models work well? Which don't?" (All these questions are part of the "Constructing an Argument" conversation.) The students respond that their models still do not do a good job of explaining the height of the Moon above the

Earth's horizon each day, but they do show how the phases of the Moon occur. He asks them to do more reading in the library to help them make their models even more consistent with how the Moon behaves (returning to the "Organizing What We Know" conversation).

As a final assessment, Mr. Gilbert asks students to look at the activities the class had completed and record in a summary table all the evidence that supports or refutes the class model of the phases of the Moon. While his students complete this task outside of class, Mr. Gilbert uses the final two days of the unit to explore with his students the classic debates about the Earth-centered versus Sun-centered models of the solar system and the evidence that Copernicus and Galileo used to support their explanatory model (an extension of the "Constructing an Argument" conversation into historical episodes).

---

[1]This vignette is paraphrased from National Research Council (NRC). 2000. *Inquiry and the national science education standards: A guide for teaching and learning*. Washington, DC: National Academy Press.

## Vignette 2. Studying Asthma in Young People

Ms. Thompson teaches 10th-grade biology in an urban high school. Her students come from working class families, and most of them have at least one family member or friend with some sort of respiratory illness. In planning a unit on the human body, Ms. Thompson thought she could "hook" students on studying asthma to better understand the influences of the environment on the body.

Ms. Thompson opened the unit by showing her students newspaper articles of how the rate of local children hospitalized with asthma had risen by more than 25% over the past 10 years. Students immediately began to ask questions: "Is asthma genetic?" "Is asthma triggered by outdoor pollution or indoor conditions?" "Can we do something about the rates of asthma in our neighborhoods?"

The students' first task was to sketch out on poster board different sources of pollution that students believed could trigger asthma attacks (beginning the "Organizing What We Know" conversation). When they had completed their drawings, Ms. Thompson noticed that they were aware of many sources of pollution, but that these were all outdoor examples—most students included pictures of industrial sources and their own school buses.

The next day Ms. Thompson distributed public service announcements from the Centers for Disease Control and Prevention that outlined common triggers for asthma attacks, including some indoor sources (dust, mold, cold air). These information sources included details about how studies on asthma were conducted (e.g., the sample populations, types of data collected, methods of analysis). Ms. Thompson then asked students to form small groups to specialize in one of these triggers and to find evidence-based information that could be presented to the class. Students were asked not only to share information, but to describe the strength of the evidence for the claims in the studies they cited. This prompted a discussion about what is meant by "convincing evidence" (the "Constructing an Argument" conversation using existing data; see Sidebar 5).

A couple of days later, as students shared their findings, they were surprised to discover that their own neighborhoods had the highest rates of asthma in the city and that the causes of these asthma attacks were not well understood. From their background readings, the students then developed a class concept map of the triggers for asthma attacks (elaborating on the "Organizing What We Know" conversation). From this tentative model (see Figure 1.4), students noticed that one possible trigger, $NO_2$, was an air pollutant produced by factories, but also produced in homes when people used their ovens.

Sidebar 5

Notice here that the "Constructing an Argument" conversation does not have to take place at the end of an inquiry. The order of these conversations is contingent on student interest and opportunity.

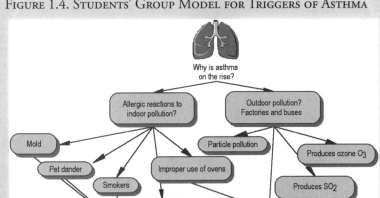

FIGURE 1.4. STUDENTS' GROUP MODEL FOR TRIGGERS OF ASTHMA

Several students commented that they knew people in poor neighborhoods who heated their homes in the winter by keeping their ovens on all night. Other students proposed that exposure to cigarette smoke was the cause of the high rates of asthma. Ms. Thompson asked her students to decide what kind of data they would need to collect to test these different hypotheses (initiating the "Generating a Model" conversation).

As a class, the students decided to create an anonymous survey about conditions in homes that could lead to asthma attacks and distribute it to all 200 students in their sophomore class. Before writing questions for the surveys, Ms. Thompson asked students to imagine taking the responses and putting that data in a table. She asked, "What would this table look like?" "Are you asking yes/no questions about smokers in the house? the number of people in the house who smoke? where they smoke?" "What kind of data analysis would each of these different kinds of data allow you to make?" (pressing students on the "Seeking Evidence" conversation).

After students found and fixed flaws in their questioning strategies, the final surveys were distributed. As the surveys were returned, students interested in testing the hypothesis about smoking decided to correlate the number of cigarettes smoked in the house with the number of asthma incidents of residents in the past month. They put their findings into a scatterplot and found a modest but significant correlation. The group testing the oven hypothesis found that only five respondents had indicated their family used ovens to heat their homes, so they felt their findings were inconclusive.

Ms. Thompson then asked students to present final arguments to their peers and for everyone to play a role in critiquing the claims (includes all students in the "Constructing an Argument" conversation). When those presenting the smoking hypothesis concluded that their evidence was strong—that exposure to cigarette smoke caused asthma attacks—several students in the audience asked why they believed this was a causal relationship and not just a correlation. When Ms. Thompson asked if there were any alternative explanations for their findings, one group of students noted that in the surveys, many of those respondents who said they smoked also said that they placed plastic on their windows during the winter to keep the house warm. These students then suggested that rates of smoking also correlated with keeping homes sealed up and that lack of air circulation may be a complicating factor in deciding what actually causes asthma attacks.

For a final assessment, Ms. Thompson asked her students to write individual proposals for a follow-up investigation that would take into account findings from their current study and disentangle correlation from causation with regard to exposure to cigarette smoke and the triggering of asthma attacks.

These vignettes provide just two examples of students creating and critiquing evidence-based explanations of how the world works. If any investigation in which students have the opportunity to engage in these four conversations can be considered a core inquiry experience, then a wide variety of circumstances exist in which this experience can happen. Students, for example, might use existing databases to pose and answer questions; they could also use computer-based simulations to generate and analyze data. In other cases, teachers could set up conditions for thought experiments in which students discuss what-if scenarios. An example would be presenting a food web diagram and asking, "What if this species of plant were to die out? What would be the impact on the rest of the system?" Students could also deconstruct claims and arguments of existing scientific reports written in nontechnical terms. Finally, long-term projects can provide rich contexts for authentic inquiry. A problem like "How does run-off from agricultural land affect local aquatic ecosystems?" can be of such scope that it contains numerous opportunities for empirical investigations (e.g., determining the effects of a single chemical on one species of macro-invertebrate in a pond).

# Family 2: Activities That Support the Core Work of Inquiry

In addition to the core work of inquiry previously described, many other types of classroom activities are often referred to as inquiry. These, however, may be better thought of as *supporting activities* of inquiry. Supporting activities prepare students to participate more meaningfully in the core activities of inquiry by acquainting them with necessary concepts, ideas, and skills. Here are some examples:

- Conducting background library/internet research.

- Watching teacher-led demonstrations.

- Performing lab-practicals where one identifies natural materials or features (e.g., rocks, xylem versus phloem in plant stems, different gases).

- Engaging in exercises to "make something happen" (e.g., convection currents in an aquarium, an acid-base reaction).

- Designing/building machines or other technologies.

- Learning the use of equipment or lab procedures.

These supporting activities can contribute to students' abilities to engage in the core conversations of inquiry. Too often, however, these are treated as the inquiry itself. Students might, for example, learn to replicate the experiments of others but never design their own, or they might do library research on current scientific controversies without ever getting to argue about evidence *they* have generated in support of a hypothesis. Part of good teaching is knowing when and how the supporting activities can contribute to students' conversations about the core knowledge-building activities of science.

# Family 3: Common Practices That Need to Be Reconsidered

Many teachers already engage their students in a range of interesting activities. These practices could be considered good starting points from which to move toward more authentic forms of inquiry. Although each of the common practices described here have some shortcomings, they can be modified to become more like the core knowledge-building practices of Family 1.

First, a word about the "scientific method." Science textbooks have placed much emphasis on this formula (making observations, defining the problem, constructing hypotheses, experimenting, analyzing results, drawing conclusions), but most scientists say it is a misrepresentation of the way science really works. First, within the traditional scientific method, questions are often based on what is interesting or doable, but they are not grounded in any coherent model. As a result, school science investigations are often uninformed and without content (e.g., experiments to determine which paper towels hold the most water). Data from these experiments are then analyzed to determine only how outcomes are related to conditions (e.g., whether small crystals of sugar will dissolve faster in water than large sugar crystals), but underlying explanations (how molecular motion helps break the chemical bonds of sugar) are rarely addressed (Chinn and Malhotra 2002; Driver et al. 1996).

The second flaw is related to the first: Because the scientific method has no provisions for students to develop an initial model to inform their questions, there can be no argument at the end of the inquiry about how their evidence fits the model. The third problem with the scientific method is that it often promotes experimentation as the only method of investigating the world (where there is a comparison between a control group and a manipulated experimental group). In science fields such as geology, field biology, natural history, and astronomy, controlled experiments are all but impossible—yet scientists in these fields all use systematic collection of data and coordination of evidence to propose explanations.

A collective reliance on oversimplified formulas for inquiry learning has given rise to some classroom practices that need to be reconsidered. Here are four examples:

*Investigating arbitrary questions.* Science inquiry does not involve questions such as "Will my bean plants grow faster listening to rock and roll music or classical music?" A question like this, although testable, has little to do with the development of any coherent understanding of underlying causes.

*Investigations outside the bounds of the natural world.* School science includes the broad domains of physics, biology, Earth and space sciences, and chemistry. It does not investigate questions of human behavior, such as, "How many students prefer pizza versus tacos for lunch?" or "Does extrasensory perception really exist?" Although these can be motivational hooks for students, they are essentially inquiries without content.

*Cookbook investigations.* Some activities are so rigidly scripted that students do not have to employ any reasoning skills—all they have to do is follow instructions. Students can, in fact, get passing grades in these activities without having a clue about the meaning of the work they are doing. Such confirmatory exercises can have a legitimate role when students have no previous inquiry experiences at all to draw upon, but a steady diet of these will soon cause students' enthusiasm for science to wither away.

*Substituting isolated process skills for complete inquiries.* From the research on learning, there is little evidence that process skills (observing, classifying, measuring, predicting, hypothesizing, inferring, and so forth) learned in isolation help students understand the purpose of these skills or how they should be used in real investigations. Inquiry should instead be treated as a *coordinated set* of activities and *taught as a whole*. Inquiry should be kept complex, but the teacher should scaffold students' efforts as needed.

# Conclusion

School science inquiry was presented here as a persuasive enterprise based on four interrelated conversations in which students engage. These conversations link models, hypotheses, evidence, and argument, but more to the point for students, they help answer the question, "Why are we doing this activity?" The aim of doing more authentic science in schools is not to mimic scientists, but to develop the depth of content knowledge, the habits of mind, and the critical reasoning skills that are so crucial to basic science literacy.

Framing inquiry as a set of conversations means that teachers will need to be skilled in orchestrating productive discussion in the classroom. They will have to encourage a climate for conversation, pay close attention to students' ideas, scaffold complex activities, and assess the intellectual development of students as they learn to "talk science." On a more systemic level, it will require that schools measure the rigor of a curriculum not by the sheer quantity of topics addressed but by the in-depth understanding sought through an engagement with a limited number of key ideas in science.

The ideas presented in this chapter challenge common beliefs about what passes as inquiry in science classrooms. For teachers interested in changing their practice, the most effective way to begin is to join like-minded colleagues to discuss the inquiry framework outlined here ("How does this framework differ from how we understand inquiry?"), analyze how inquiry is currently being practiced in their classrooms ("Where does our current practice fit into the 'families' of inquiry presented here?" "Are there elements of these four conversations that already take place in our curriculum?"), and then ask how they might support one another in adapting practice to include the core knowledge-building practices of science ("How could we systematically foster these kinds of conversations about questions, models, data, evidence, and argument?").

As you read the following chapters in this book, consider how the images of inquiry presented in this chapter reappear in creative and dynamic ways.

# Historical Development of Teaching Science as Inquiry

# 2

**Eugene L. Chiappetta, University of Houston**

O ver the past 200 years, science teaching in the United States has evolved from conveying science as a body of knowledge to a more learner-centered approach, generally referred to as teaching science as inquiry. This latter approach challenges students to form deep understandings about natural phenomena by engaging in the construction of scientific knowledge through an active process of investigation.

Secondary school science teaching today should be initiated by focusing on scientific theories and models, asking researchable questions, generating hypotheses, gathering information, presenting evidence, and forming arguments—that is, by thinking, investigating, and talking science. This approach can be supported and complemented when students hone their investigative skills and teachers stress the applications of science and discuss the history and nature of science.

This chapter examines four periods in the history of science education. In particular it looks at how societal pressures brought about the teaching of science as inquiry in each period and how educators, cognitive psychologists, and scientists have responded with recommendations appearing in national science education reform documents. In addition, this review looks at the influence of scientists on the content and process of scientific inquiry and the contribution of cognitive psychologists to student-centered learning.

# The Emergence of Teaching Science as Inquiry

## The Period From the Early 1800s to 1915

During the early 1800s the United States was building a nation. Cities were small and most people lived in rural areas. Secondary schools were in their infancy, attended only by the privileged in preparation for college. The few science courses offered in high schools stressed the practical sides of science and technology, such as astronomical calculations, navigation, mensuration (measurement), and surveying. After 1860 many high school curricula included botany, meteorology, mineralogy, physiology, and zoology. Science courses in the mid- to late 1800s were descriptive and included little or no laboratory work. Many individuals who were teaching science lacked a strong background in science. Didactic instruction was the teaching standard, and science was taught primarily as a body of factual information.

At this time, college science programs, because of college entrance requirements, directly influenced high school biology, chemistry, and physics courses. High school science teaching began to emulate college and university instruction, with little attention paid to students' interests or the need to understand the environment. High school science courses became watered-down college science courses in which teachers covered many textbook chapters, implementing a laboratory exercise now and then. These courses stressed science as content, with little attention given to investigation or technology; they rarely reflected on how scientific work is conducted. Late in the 19th century, however, national committees recognized the domination of high school science by college science teaching and sought to change the situation.

The Committee of Ten (Committee on Secondary School Studies 1893) proposed to standardize the high school curriculum. In a report, the committee asserted that secondary schools did not exist for the sole purpose of educating our youth for college. The report also recommended a better alignment of programs from elementary through high school. The report had the effect of decreasing the influence of colleges on some high school science courses. However, even with more science courses offered in the secondary school—some for the college-bound students and some for those not college bound—students were still not learning science through investigation.

Two trends in high school science emerged during the late 1800s and early 1900s. One was an emphasis on having students learn the applications they would need to function in an industrial society. The other trend stressed preparation for college science, which, as we know, was content heavy and didactic. In 1915, the Central Association of Science and Mathematics Teachers, convening on the national level, stressed that students should be taught the methods for obtaining accurate information.

# The Period From 1915 to 1955

During the first half of the 20th century, many significant events—for example, World War I, the influenza pandemic, the Great Depression, and World War II—brought about political and social pressures that shaped the goals of public school education. School science programs stressed the practical aspect of science so that students could take their place as productive members of society. Although teaching science continued to emphasize factual information with some practical application, the process of science and the term *inquiry* began to appear in national committee recommendations and the research literature.

From about 1910 to 1930 the student population grew rapidly in the United States, as did the establishment of the grades 1–6, 7–9, 10–12 pattern of school organization. This situation brought about curriculum innovation and a broadening of the aims of science education, which were noted in the following general goal statements from the Commission on the Reorganization of Secondary Education (1918): (1) health, (2) command of fundamental process, (3) worthy home membership, (4) vocation, (5) citizenship, (6) worthy use of leisure time, and (7) ethical character. A report on secondary school science issued in 1920 reinforced these aims by encouraging science educators to incorporate them into science teaching, especially in general science and biology (Caldwell 1920).

However, a 1924 report from the Committee on the Place of Science in Education of the American Association for the Advancement of Science emphasized the importance of scientific thinking as a goal of science teaching; the report urged moving science instruction toward an inquiry-based approach (Caldwell 1924). The report stressed the importance of observation and experimentation, with the intent of giving students a better feeling for the scientific enterprise. In effect the scientific community was saying to educators that school science needed to be more than teaching about the content of science; it also had to be about science as a way of thinking and investigating. This was a significant addition to the existing lists of science education goals.

Then in 1934 the Commission on Secondary Curriculum of the Progressive Education Association issued a report stressing the importance of reflective thinking in science, of focusing the curriculum on content that would be useful in students' lives, and of correlating life's problems with the curriculum (Progressive Education Association 1938).

One individual who had a great deal to say about the functional aspect of knowledge, scientific inquiry, and problem solving was John Dewey (1859–1952)—a philosopher, psychologist, and education reformer who held a pragmatic view of education. Dewey (1938), a leader of the progressive movement, stressed learning by doing and was opposed to learning simply for the sake of gaining knowledge. He was a proponent of learning the process of inquiry and of solving problems that were important to society and relevant to students.

Dewey believed that the development of the individual and the betterment of society should be the aims of education. He also believed that students should learn and use the scientific method rather than merely learn the core concepts of science. Scientific knowledge and especially "the method of science" were tools to enrich the lives of students.

Despite various recommendations from national committees to incorporate student inquiry into the science curriculum during the first half of the 20th century, few of the recommendations were ever implemented widely in science classrooms throughout the United States (Bybee 1977).

# The Period From 1955 to 1980

The United States entered into a new era after World War II. During the 1950s and 1960s, the nation shifted from a war economy to a period of economic expansion and population growth, with many soldiers returning to civilian life, starting families, and raising children. The need for housing, schools, and transportation increased greatly. At the same time, the United States entered into a long Cold War with the Soviet Union, a situation that demanded military preparedness as well as scientific and technological advancement.

In the early to mid-1950s critics voiced concern about the state of public education. Mathematicians and scientists were especially critical, noting that students were not going into mathematics and science and that their high school courses were out of date and out of line with those two disciplines. "The courses, [mathematicians and scientists] claimed, lacked rigor, were dogmatically taught, were content oriented, lacked conceptual unity, were outdated, and had little bearing on what was happening in the scientific disciplines" (Collette and Chiappetta 1989, pp. 11–12). University mathematicians and scientists found that students entering college were poorly prepared to study their subjects.

Although science and mathematics curriculum reforms were under way by the mid-1950s, the launching of the first space satellite, *Sputnik,* in 1957 by the Russians incited a massive curriculum reform program in U.S. science and mathematics education. The space satellite signaled that the Soviet Union was more advanced in science and technology than the United States, supporting earlier warnings that the U.S. education system was falling behind. The reforms brought about many changes and innovations in K–12 science curriculum materials; curriculum specialists, teachers, scientists, and mathematicians all played a role in these reforms.

One such reformer was Joseph Schwab (1909–1988), a contributor to the innovative Biological Sciences Curriculum Study (BSCS) high school biology course materials, who advanced our understanding of inquiry-based instruction. He enrolled in the university at age 15, earning undergraduate degrees in English and physics and later a doctorate in genetics (Westbury and Wilkof 1978). Schwab worked at the University of Chicago for over 50 years, where John Dewey had set up the Lab School and where educator Ralph Tyler (1902–1994) became well-known for his work in curriculum development.

The phrase "teaching science as enquiry" is conspicuous in a 1962 lecture by Schwab at Harvard University titled "The Teaching of Science as Enquiry." Schwab preferred the use of *enquiry* to *inquiry,* because he disagreed with the ideas surrounding inquiry then being promoted, especially by psychologists. His idea of enquiry instruction was to teach students about the major paradigms of science, that is, the manner in which a certain community of scientists view a major idea and the way they investigate it. In his lecture, Schwab urged science educators to stress the conceptions of science and how they change over time. He placed a premium on how scientists view the ideas (content) they are developing and how these ideas shape what scientists do and say about the data they collect. Science should not be viewed as dogma, he said, but as revisionary and fluid. Teachers misrepresent science when they present it as a rhetoric of conclusion or as a finished product. He urged that students be active in the laboratory and that they develop their critical thinking skills by analyzing the works and original papers of scientists.

Around the same time, learning psychologist David Ausubel (1918– )(1963) advocated meaningful verbal learning, saying that science subject matter should be presented in a manner accessible to students. Learners, he said, will incorporate meaningful content into their knowledge bases, while they will quickly forget information learned by rote. Learning, Ausubel stressed, must begin with what the student knows, an assertion also made by today's constructivists and cognitive psychologists.

Jerome Bruner (1915– ) (1961), on the other hand, was a staunch advocate of "learning by discovery." He believed that the main purpose of education was to teach students how to learn rather than to simply accumulate information. Bruner held that there were four benefits of discovery learning: the increase of intellectual potency, the shift from extrinsic to intrinsic rewards, the heuristics of discovery, and the aid to the memory process. Bruner believed that by not feeding students explanations, teachers would encourage students to figure things out for themselves. Bruner's writings were used to promote the discovery and process approaches to science teaching.

Another major contributor to the evolution of science teaching was Jean Piaget (1896–1980), the most well-known developmental psychologist of his time. According to Piaget, intellectual development occurs through the construction of thinking skills (logical structures) that develop through experiences that challenge the learner to figure out puzzling events. Piaget's so-called concrete operational abilities (e.g., ordering, classifying, using numbers, and conserving mass) and formal operational abilities (e.g., combinatorial reasoning, proportional reasoning, controlling variables, and hypothetical reasoning) corresponded well with the science process skills that were the emphasis of the science process movement of the 1960s and 1970s.

It should be noted that not all science educators advocated the learning methods of inquiry science, largely because these methods lacked an emphasis on content. During the 1970s, Driver and Easley (1978) cautioned science educators not to give too much attention to learners' logical structures of thought and the data-gathering process involved in scientific investigation; they recommended giving more attention to conceptual frameworks of substantive knowledge. These researchers stressed the importance of getting students to think about and discuss their own ideas of phenomena and the importance of focusing on students' misconceptions and preconceptions.

The period from 1955 to 1980 was the golden era of science curriculum reform in the United States, supported by large government funding in response to the scientific ascendancy of the Soviet Union. Government-sponsored textbook programs for high school science contained more up-to-date science content than did commercial textbooks. Further, textbooks that came out of those programs promoted inquiry-based instruction. Many papers, articles, and books of the time stressed the importance of involving students in learning how to do science.

As the result of Joseph Schwab's writings and curriculum work, teaching science as inquiry became a popular approach in the science education community. Inquiry science was promoted in high school, with an emphasis on work in the laboratory, in the belief that this strategy would teach students about the processes of science at the same time that it advanced their content knowledge. Unfortunately, the reform efforts did not reach all high schools in the country and the reform movement was not sustained by government funding. In addition, student achievement and interest in science was on the decline.

## The Period From 1980 to 2006

During the 1980s, science education again came under criticism for not preparing youth to take their place in a scientific and technological society. Japan was becoming a formidable competitor in the world economy, particularly in the manufacture of automobiles, electronic equipment, and steel. Again, the United States felt threatened by another country, and the education system was called on to become part of the solution. This time it was an economic threat, which called forth a report titled *A Nation at Risk* from the National Commission on Excellence in Education (1983): "Our education system has fallen behind and this is reflected in our leadership in commerce, industry, science and technological innovations, which is being taken over by competitors throughout the world" (p. 5). As a result, many other reports were issued on the state of education, some of which were funded by the National Science Foundation.

A document by Project Synthesis summarized thousands of pages of reports from professional organizations on the state of science education (Harms and Yager 1981). The report recommended four goal clusters for science education: personal needs, societal issues, academic preparation, and career education. This orientation stressed the needs of students and the relationship among science, technology, and society, thus creating a better balance of science education goals than those that placed a heavy emphasis on pure science. The core content areas of science and teaching science as inquiry would take a lesser role in science education, especially at the middle school level. In the late 1970s and during the 1980s, an attempt was made to take up a progressive movement in science education that saw social issues and values education as important goals (DeBoer 2000).

During the 1990s two reports appeared that set out to reform science education throughout the nation, with the intent of reaching all students in grades K–12. The first was *Science for All Americans: Project 2061* (AAAS 1990) and the second was *National Science Education Standards* (NRC 1996).

The goal of Project 2061 was to produce a scientifically literate society by the year 2061. Its mottos were "science for all students" and "less is more." The document stressed student understanding of the nature of science, mathematics, and technology and how these enterprises function separately and together. Students should gain not only an understanding of the core concepts of the disciplines but also historical and contemporary perspectives of them. Leaders of the project sought to develop students' curiosity and inclination to find out. However, the committee made no attempt to prescribe ways in which students should be taught science because there are many approaches to effective science instruction. Therefore, the translation of the Project 2061 goals were taken up by another group that produced national standards and called attention to the importance of inquiry in the science classroom.

The National Science Education Standards (NSES) (NRC 1996) gave high priority to inquiry-based science teaching, using the phrase "teaching science as inquiry" throughout. The importance of inquiry in the NSES is stated as follows:

> *Scientific inquiry refers to the diverse ways in which scientists study the natural world and propose explanations based on the evidence derived from their work. Inquiry also refers to the activities of students in which they develop knowledge and understanding of scientific ideas, as well as an understanding of how scientists study the natural world.*

> *Inquiry is a multifaceted activity that involves making observations; posing questions; examining books and other sources of information to see what is already known; planning investigations; reviewing what is already known in light of experimental evidence; using tools to gather, analyze, and interpret data; proposing answers, explanations, and predictions; and communicating the*

*results. Inquiry requires identification of assumptions, use of critical and logical thinking, and consideration of alternative explanations. . . .*

*Although the Standards emphasize inquiry, this should not be interpreted as recommending a single approach to science teaching. Teachers should use different strategies to develop the knowledge, understanding, and abilities described in the content standards. Conducting hands-on science activities does not guarantee inquiry, nor is reading about science incompatible with inquiry. . . .*
(NRC 1996, p. 23)

A companion volume to the NSES, published in 2000, was *Inquiry and the National Science Education Standards* (NRC 2000). It provides teachers with many examples of inquiry-based instruction in many settings, from the classroom to the school grounds and into the community. In the foreword, Bruce Alberts, president of the National Academy of Sciences, wrote, "Students need to learn the principles and concepts of science, acquire the reasoning and procedural skills of scientists, and understand the nature of science as a particular form of human endeavor" (NRC 2000, p. xiii). *Inquiring Into Inquiry Learning and Teaching in Science* (Minstrell and van Zee 2000) similarly informed educators about inquiry-based science instruction.

The field of cognitive psychology has grown significantly since the 1980s, providing educators with important insights into teaching and learning science (e.g., Bransford, Brown, and Cocking 2000). The current cognitive approach encourages teachers to focus on what students know about the subject under study and to begin instruction with the intent of teaching for deeper understanding. High school science teachers must actively engage students in studying natural phenomena within familiar contexts and situations, which often extend beyond the science laboratory into the home and community. Deep understanding of natural phenomena and scientific inquiry must become a primary goal of the curriculum. In addition, students must be encouraged to monitor their own understanding of scientific content and process, noting how these ideas change during learning.

# What Have We Learned From the Past?

The history of science education over the past 200 years illustrates why national committees have been assembled to initiate reform. The pressure to change school science stems from political forces to make the nation more economically productive, militarily prepared, and physically healthy. A recurrent recommendation from national committees has been to expand the traditional mode of science teaching from one that stresses teaching science as a body of knowledge to one that stresses the development of fundamental scientific knowledge through inquiry-based learning.

Currently, science education stresses the importance of students developing a deep understanding of core scientific knowledge and the methods of science. The learning must encourage students to think and talk more like scientists. Although not all forms of instruction can be labeled teaching science as inquiry, this approach can be supported and complemented by other types of instruction in which investigative skills are refined, the applications of science are stressed, the history of science studied, and the nature of science discussed. Planning for this type of curriculum can also address students' needs and interests, perhaps better than a course of study centering primarily on the development of fundamental concepts and principles.

The challenge has never been greater for secondary school science teachers to understand, plan, and implement the science-as-inquiry approach—an approach that attempts to assimilate the recommendations of many professional committees while accommodating the pressures of a changing society.

## Acknowledgments

I wish to thank Alfred Collette for providing me with a good foundation of the history of science education and Ian Westbury for giving me a better perspective of Joseph Schwab's thinking regarding teaching science as enquiry.

# Inquiry in the Earth Sciences

3

Eric J. Pyle, James Madison University

Teaching Earth science in the K–12 classroom presents a challenge compared to other sciences in the curriculum. Earth science is an interdisciplinary science, encompassing ideas from physics, chemistry, and biology but applied through geology, meteorology, oceanography, and, in K–12 curricula, space science and astronomy. Earth science is not a narrow set of ideas, but a synthesis of many ideas in science.

Inquiry experiences in the Earth sciences are often indirect, because direct experimentation, such as is used in the physical sciences, is typically not possible. Because of the natural variability of Earth materials, their broad but often interrupted (or missing) distribution, and the extended time spans required for Earth processes to operate, controlling all of the variables and representing real-world conditions in a laboratory are often difficult. As a result, many teachers avoid inquiry altogether in Earth science classes.

To support inquiry in the Earth sciences it is important to consider the components of inquiry. In this chapter, I describe a model that can guide investigations in the Earth science classroom and addresses these components. Throughout the chapter I use different examples but most are geologic in nature. Given the tendency to emphasize geology content in Earth science courses, these examples may be more familiar to those teaching Earth science than to teachers in other science areas.

# Components of Inquiry: A Framework

Inquiries in Earth science should provide experiences with science that allow students to ask questions, collect and analyze data, and discuss their conclusions (see NRC 1996). These three broad components can be simply stated as (a) defining questions, (b) selecting methods, and (c) arriving at solutions (Monk and Dillon 1995). Even though the compoents are distinct areas, they are linked together by a concept, problem, or event. In terms of Earth science, the question that guides each type of inquiry can be interdisciplinary or it can reside in one specific content area in Earth science. Once the question is identified, then appropriate methods based on observation or model building can be developed. The findings from this step result in creating solutions, which offers new understanding about phenomena. Ultimately, the complexity of the inquiry depends on the topic selected and the amount of time allocated for the inquiry. An overall view of this framework is depicted in Figure 3.1.

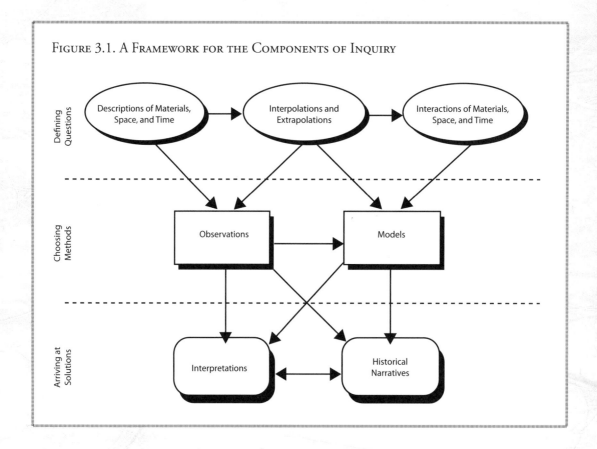

FIGURE 3.1. A FRAMEWORK FOR THE COMPONENTS OF INQUIRY

# Defining Questions That Make Sense in Earth Science

*An issue that 8th-grade Earth science teacher Ms. Spurrier has always struggled with is getting her students to understand the relationship between landforms and the rock structures beneath the land surface. Her students can identify folds and faults on a test without problem, but they cannot transfer this knowledge to mountains, stream drainage patterns, or landslides. During a topographic map reading exercise, one of her students asks her why the river channels on some maps look like the branches in a leaf, while on other maps the pattern looks like steps or ladders. Ms. Spurrier decides that she can structure a student investigation around maps on which she can place known faults and ridges of resistant rock (e.g., sandstone). The question she poses to her students is this: "What do faults and rocks have to do with the course of rivers?"*

Inquiries in the Earth sciences are not necessarily about making generalizable statements that go beyond a setting. They can also consist of describing an event that represents a setting and then comparing descriptions to different settings (Ault 1998). Either inquiry form is important in describing natural phenomena. The real challenge in Earth science inquiries is to frame questions in terms of (a) *materials*, such as rocks, minerals, and water, (b) *space*, or where the materials are found or how they are distributed, and (c) *time*, or how materials and their distributions have or will change and evolve. When these three areas are included in an Earth science question, there is a sense that phenomena to be explored are complex, interactive, and uncontrollable and therefore difficult to investigate in a laboratory setting that stresses control.

At the simplest level, meaningful questions in Earth science center on *descriptions*. In the classroom, these questions tend to result in the classification, comparison, or quantification of materials. Space is often added as location, such as where certain minerals can be found, while time can be a matter of suggesting a sequence that is forward or backward in time. These positions, however, are not clearly delineated and can vary with the conceptual orientations of the question.

In moving from descriptions to *interpolations* and *extrapolations,* more questions, including more complex questions, can be asked. Questions of interpolation describe materials that may have been changed or removed by Earth processes, while questions of extrapolations can describe what materials will look like in different conditions. In either orientation, there is reliance on visualizations, such as maps, charts, scales, photographs, and graphs.

Another dimension of questions pertains to *interactions.* Descriptions, inter-polations, and extrapolations fall short of providing a full, causal explanation of Earth phenomena. Questions that focus on interactions come even closer to defining Earth phenomena. Yet an increase in complexity makes it harder to find enough data and time to pursue the question meaningfully in the class-room. Ultimately, such questions can serve as a driving course or unit ques-tion and be based within a "sphere": lithosphere, hydrosphere, atmosphere, or cryosphere. Questions bounded by a sphere can ultimately allow students to engage in inquiry that permits a fuller understanding of Earth phenomena.

In the vignette at the beginning of this section, Ms. Spurrier posed an in-terpolation question structured around an interaction between the orienta-tion of materials and the pattern that streams assume over a larger area. In doing this, her question addressed the important components of materials, space, and time. The inquiry lesson emerging from the student's question was focused on a specific concept and corresponded to material students were struggling with in class. Ms. Spurrier could have easily discussed this topic during a class period, but she elected to provide a learning opportunity that placed phenomena in the middle of the lesson. This strategy allowed students to construct their knowledge about this topic. Other sample questions are posed in Table 3.1.

# Selecting Methods in Earth Science— Observations and Models

*Ms. Spurrier and her students cannot help but observe that the day after a heavy rainstorm her classroom is filled with an overpowering stench. Yet the stream that flows next to the building is usually barely flowing at all. The problem only be-came apparent after the growth of the nearby subdivision. Besides the obvious problem the smell represents, Ms. Spurrier decides that this phenomenon is one that her students can investigate.*

*As a part setting up the investigation, Ms. Spurrier has her students list factors they believe have caused or are related to the problem. Her students have identified such factors as the amount of rainfall, the frequency of heavy rainfalls, the size of the stream channel, and the number of houses in the subdivision. One student also asks whether the houses are attached to a public sewer line or use septic tanks.*

*There are obvious public health issues to which Ms. Spurrier does not wish to expose her students, so she structures the inquiry carefully. She selects a time when it hasn't*

**TABLE 3.1. SAMPLE EARTH SCIENCE INQUIRY QUESTIONS**

| Description | • What is the maximum elevation of the Sun at noon during the school year? |
| | • What is the role of grain size in the settling rates of sediment in a column of water? |
| | • What do the minerals that are present in metamorphic rocks tell us about the temperatures and pressures at which the rock formed? |
| **Interpolations and Extrapolations** | • From the data provided, construct a graph that shows the negative relationship between grain size and rate of cooling for molten rock. |
| | • Using temperature data for the past several winters, generate a prediction for next winter. |
| | • What does a geologic map of the Moon tell us about its history? |
| **Interactions** | • How are the deposits left by glaciers and alluvial fans different? |
| | • In what ways are grain sorting and grain size related to the environment in which a rock forms? |
| | • What would a change in the trade winds do to ocean currents? |

*rained for several days to have students take careful measurements of the size and depth of the channel and what they see in the channel. She also assigns students to research the factors they have previously identified (see above paragraph). Using these pieces of information, the class constructs a map showing the school grounds, the stream, and the subdivision. Using rainfall data from the local television station, they construct a model that suggests that if the rainfall is over 2 cm then the room will smell awful the next day. All they need is a heavy rain to test their model.*

Unlike investigations in physics or chemistry, the methods in Earth science seldom include the direct manipulation of variables, except in the context of simulating an Earth process under laboratory conditions. The same is true for historical investigations as well as for those in the classroom. For the most part, Earth science investigations and inquiries are based on observations about an Earth event, using models to test supported explanations.

Observations in Earth science are more than just verbal descriptions. Were observations limited to measurements of grain size, magnitude of brightness, intensity of the storm, or geometric relations of folds and faults, they would be largely indistinguishable from measurements of force, voltage, pH, or concentration. What separates observations in Earth science from other disciplines is the need to consider a range of scales, whether such scales are in the thickness of the rind on a weathered rock, the magnitude of a flood, or the large-scale map patterns of ocean currents. Such observations are essentially identical, whether the observations are determined by high-tech tools (such as satellite imagery and GIS map layers) or more traditional tools (such as pocket transits and hand lenses or magnifiers).

Manipulating how observations are made, however, usually requires a model of some sort with variables that can be changed. Models are dependent on the overlap or cumulative effect of different factors, as well as on the boundary conditions occurring in the model. For instance, describing an eruption of a volcano requires observations of the temperature of the lava, the amount of different chemical elements, and the amount of gas in the lava. If any of these variables changes, a different eruption will result, which frequently happens within the same volcano over time.

Models of use in explaining Earth phenomena tend to fall into one of four categories, according to Stevens and Collins (1980):

1. Simulation—Duplication in how the materials change when conditions are changed is carried out (e.g., when samples of limestone are immersed in different concentrations of HCl to duplicate how rocks containing $CaCO_3$ chemically weather).

2. Functional—Measurement is used to make interpolations or extrapolations (e.g., deciding how long a sedimentary layer took to accumulate based on how fast different sediments settle).

3. Cyclical—Connections between specific materials are explored (e.g., the behavior of solid Earth materials over time in the rock cycle).

4. Global/Systems—Interpretation are made based on observations of complex phenomena (e.g., the relationship of rock types to plate margins).

In an instructional sense, it is important to ensure that students know when one type of model or another is appropriate, what model components are or can be determined in the context of the question of interest, and how various models for an Earth phenomenon can be compared and contrasted. In answering these questions, models can become more or less sophisticated, with students learning through the refinement of the model. (Chapter 1 includes an expanded discussion about models.)

In their investigation of the odor in the classroom, Ms. Spurrier guided her students in an inquiry requiring them to make or collect observations and use them in the context of a functional model. What the students sometimes find in their investigation is that without sufficient observations no single model best fits their data. In Ms. Spurrier's class, the real cause of the problem turned out to be the subdivision's water treatment plant, which had failed due to an increased load of influent wastewater without an increase in the processing capacity of the plant. Heavy rainfall caused the plant to overflow. Examples of other inquiry methods are listed in Table 3.2.

TABLE 3.2. SAMPLE EARTH SCIENCE INQUIRY METHODS

| Observations | • Determining the direction of ocean currents with increasing depth, starting at the surface.<br><br>• Comparing the angles between the faces of different-size crystals of the same material.<br><br>• Determining the permeability of different rocks by immersion in water for different amounts of time. |
|---|---|
| Models | • Estimating cloud base altitude, based on temperature, dew point, and adiabatic lapse rates.<br><br>• Using temperature trend charts for the past 100,000 years to make temperature projections for the next 20,000 years.<br><br>• Using a stream table with different types of sediment and water flow rates to characterize streams. |

# Arriving at Solutions—
# Interpretive and Historical

*Many of Ms. Spurrier's students travel to the beach on school breaks. The most popular route to the beach is right down the nearby state highway. Being a fan of the beach herself, Ms. Spurrier knows the route well, and she poses a descriptive question to her students: "Count the number of ridges you pass over or through with white sand in the road cut and the number of short, scrubby pine trees on them." When the students return from break, some students tell her they saw two or three such ridges; others saw four or five. She asks them how these ridges compared with the beach. At first, the students are a little confused. When they discuss the parts of the beach and the areas just behind the beach, however, the lights go on for some of the students. "Those sandy ridges were the beach once, weren't they?" asks one of her students.*

Given the wide range of questions tied to Earth phenomena and the methods used to define them, the next step is to decide what answers make sense. Solutions to questions in Earth science span the range from narrow, prescribed answers based on classification to a broad set of answers capturing the complex and dynamic nature of Earth systems. Yet even with the scale of solution that can be generated, it is not enough to offer a solution from a single reference point. For example, one can define a process that describes a phenomenon, such as a river flooding, but until the mechanisms producing that process are defined (such as the size of the floodplain, stream peak discharge, and peak flow duration), the solution remains incomplete.

Interpretations are types of solutions that attempt to reconcile sets of observations, with the goal of testing models. For instance, data sets from the International Ocean Drilling Program have been used in classrooms, enabling students to generate climate and temperature models for the past, based on interpretations of microfossils, sediment thickness, and oxygen isotope ratios. These same interpretations can be used to test models of paleoclimates for different regions during the Ice Age.

Another form of solution is a historical representation, which is a narrative description of the phenomenon or object of inquiry. With detailed descriptions, it is possible to contribute to a set of ideas or a larger problem of interest, or there can be the reconciliation of different descriptions of the same phenomenon by different models. Once these narratives are integrated into a larger set of ideas, they have value as a solution to a larger path of investigation. In the classroom, for example, "expert" groups of students might separately describe the same samples of materials, with each group looking at a different aspect of the materials. Using soil samples borrowed from the local soil conservation service office, one group of students might identify the soil types, another might measure the thicknesses, and a third and fourth group could plot the sample locations on a map and research the type of bedrock that underlies an area. When the data is pooled, their observations could be used to construct a history of local landform development.

Limits are imposed by the incongruity between geologic time and human time. Ms. Spurrier's students saw a great deal of sand when they went to the beach, but they needed interpretations to see those sandy ridges as past beach terraces. They also needed guidance to see that the ridges are a historical record of sea level changes. Additional solution examples are found in Table 3.3.

TABLE 3.3. SAMPLE EARTH SCIENCE INQUIRY SOLUTIONS

| Interpretations | • A determination of the relative movement along a fault plane from map pattern data.<br><br>• Description of a paleoenvironment based on rock and fossil types.<br><br>• An estimate of the past location of a continent, based, for example, on rock type, fossils, and paleomagnetic information. |
|---|---|
| Historical Representations | • A block diagram, constructed from fossils, rock types, and layer thickness from different, but nearby, locations.<br><br>• A determination of the age and timing of storm events, from grain sizes, shell fragments, ripples, etc., drawn from trenches dug in the beach.<br><br>• A reconstruction of past positions of a continent based on a regional stratigraphic column. |

# Conclusion

It should be readily apparent that even without the same level of control over the conditions of inquiry enjoyed by other sciences, inquiries in Earth science can be structured in a manner that is reflective of the nature of the various Earth sciences. Earth scientists rarely have the opportunity to either fully describe or fully control the conditions of Earth phenomena in order to study them. As a consequence, Earth science teachers need to see where the flow of learning opportunities lie, helping students see how Earth events unfold in unique combinations of materials over space and time, leading them in the use of pragmatic models and observations, and arriving at solutions that reflect both the testable interpretations needed for any science and the cumulative contributions of separate inquiries in a more narrowly defined physical area. Only when Earth science instruction is embedded in such a framework will the learning experiences for students advance beyond rote memorization of terminology and events and allow students to embrace the true and engaging complexity of Earth systems.

# Inquiry in the Chemistry Classroom: Perplexity, Model Testing, and Synthesis

4

Scott McDonald, Pennsylvania State University
Brett Criswell, Pennsylvania State University
Oliver Dreon, Jr., Cumberland Valley High School, Mechanicsburg, PA

In this chapter, we describe how the revolutionary views of Lavoisier's theory of combustion proposed in the late 1700s were used as a context for a set of interrelated, inquiry-fostering investigations in a high school chemistry class. In addition, we use this example of chemistry inquiry as a case to develop some central ideas about inquiry pedagogy in science classrooms across content areas.

The concept of teaching through inquiry has been discussed in science education for decades and has an extensive history of interpretation (see Chapter 2). In addition, there has been considerable work in the development of frameworks for analyzing science curriculum for its inquiry content. Often, however, inquiry is characterized in terms of idealized standards that focus to a large extent on the degree of student autonomy or authenticity to science practices (NRC 2000).

Understanding the value of inquiry science teaching requires looking beyond the idealized standard and into real classrooms. The question then becomes, "What are the characteristics of inquiry science teaching, and how can a description be captured to support teachers in adopting inquiry pedagogy practices?" Our approach has been to work toward a theory of teaching grounded in practice (Richardson 2000) and, specifically, to use multiple instances of classroom practice to extract elements of classroom inquiry science teaching. We frame the activities described in this chapter in terms of three elements of classroom inquiry science teaching identified from our practice: perplexity, model testing, and synthesis.

All the activities described took place in Mr. Criswell's (the second author's) 11th-grade Introductory Chemistry classroom. His overall objective for this series of lessons was for students to develop a model of combustion and recognize its relationship to slower versions of the same process (e.g., rusting). Eventually, students applied their model of combustion to explain how various common fuels burn, which included being able to represent combustion processes in the form of simple word equations.

# Perplexity

*The best, indeed the only preparation [for learning] is arousal to a perception of something that needs explanation, something unexpected, puzzling, peculiar. When the feeling of a genuine perplexity lays hold of any mind (no matter how the feeling arises), that mind is alert and inquiring.* (Dewey 1910, p. 207)

As Dewey aptly described, if we teachers want our students to engage in science in a meaningful way and develop deep conceptual understandings of phenomena, we need to engender in them a sense of perplexity. However, creating a science classroom that causes students to be perplexed without being confused is a challenging task. It is an even more daunting challenge to navigate when one considers the need to align students' classroom experiences with their everyday-life experiences. Students are accustomed to complex multithreaded plots in television shows and movies and also multiple simultaneous modes of communication (e.g., talking on the phone while e-mailing and sending instant messages). There is also evidence that more complex learning experiences aid student learning. In contrast, science curriculum tends to be linear. Students often have difficulty making connections between individual daily classroom activities and fail to understand the larger scientific concepts the teacher is using to organize all the disparate activities.

One attempt to address this difficulty is problem-based learning, where curricular activities are organized around questions developed out of an anchoring activity or event. Connecting students' learning to shared phenomena they have experienced in class helps students understand how individual activities fit into a larger conceptual pattern. Organizing activities in more multithreaded ways may help students develop a more sophisticated conception of science. There may be cognitive, motivational, and other advantages to thinking about curriculum in less linear ways. By organizing instruction in a way that contains multiple threads of activity, some subsets of which are always open for investigation and discussion, teachers can maintain a level of perplexity among their students.

In a traditional chemistry classroom, teachers may have students follow preset experimental procedures to determine known solutions or deliver lectures on differences between physical and chemical change. To develop deep conceptual understanding students must engage with empirical evidence in a way that requires them to both interpret evidence from various sources and make an argument to support a particular interpretation or model (see Chapter 8). If teachers do not engage students in a more complex version of the processes of science, they communicate implicitly that science is linear and unambiguous and has clear answers that are known not only in general but also in particular by the teacher.

Curriculum and pedagogy in science still generally approach science in a linear fashion with activities being designed as a chain, ideally organized to build conceptual understanding in a stepwise fashion from one activity to the next. Students are rarely engaged in multiple, seemingly disparate threads of activity of varying duration over long periods of time, which eventually resolve into different aspects of the same underlying phenomenon.

This type of pedagogical structure—involving complex, interwoven threads of activity—lends itself best to classroom scientific inquiry. Although individual investigations or activities may have clear results, the ways those results connect to other open or closed investigations must be determined by the students. This creates doubt about the validity of ideas and creates perplexity in the form of multiple, sometimes conflicting, activity threads that students are attempting to connect. The hard work of coming to conclusions and weighing evidence rests with the students. Mr. Criswell's lessons were designed with student perplexity in mind. Students were asked to do testing and synthesis of evidence in the context of creating a model for combustion.

The unit began with students viewing and discussing a video about spontaneous human combustion with the idea of exploring the validity of spontaneous human combustion as a scientific explanation. Mr. Criswell focused students on determining if they considered such supernatural offerings viable and scientific. Whatever the direction of this conversation, Mr. Criswell at no point offered a valid scientific alternative.

A week later students began considering the difference between physical and chemical change, beginning with the idea that chemical changes produce a new substance while physical changes do not. Using the formation (or lack of formation) of a new substance as the criterion for distinguishing between the two types of change seems straightforward. However, a pair of demonstrations made students aware that their current, limited understanding of chemistry reduced the usefulness of this criterion. Both involved color changes brought about by the addition of heat. The first involved placing a warm hand on a sheet of liquid crystals,[1] which changes from a brownish-black to various shades of green and blue; the second involved heating cobalt (II) chloride hexahydrate in a test tube with a laboratory burner, producing a change from a wine color to a royal blue.

The first color change—of the liquid crystals—is an example of a physical change brought about by a shift in the alignment or orientation of molecules with respect to each other. The second—of the cobalt (II) chloride—is a chemical change brought on by the release of water from the hydrated form. The point made was that until students' chemical understanding evolved, they would need to rely on macroscopic clues to indicate what type of change had occurred. Mr. Criswell then discussed signposts of chemical change that would be used throughout the course (i.e., dramatic energy change, color change, precipitate formation, formation of a gas, and production of an odor). These activities laid the groundwork for students engaging with models of phenomena, a critical part of classroom inquiry science.

## Model Testing

Developing arguments based on evidence is an organizing principle in the National Science Education Standards' essential features of classroom inquiry, which include questions, evidence, explanations, and justifications (NRC 2000). Windschitl (Chapter 1) suggests that argumentation in science is organized by "developing models and hypotheses and then testing them against evidence derived from observation and experiment" (p. 2). This does

---

[1] For example, product LC-2530A, available from Educational Innovations at *www.teachersource.com*

not mean having students debate different models by picking a side and defending it, as argumentation has often been misinterpreted, but is instead an empirical testing of alternative models.

For teachers to engage their students in model testing, multiple viable alternative models must be brought to the table for students to discuss and test against evidence. By drawing on the history of his discipline, specifically historical models of combustion, Mr. Criswell was able to frame his students' investigations in a historical disagreement between competing models of combustion—phlogiston theory and Lavoisier's theory.

Following the discussion of physical and chemical change, students were asked to set up an investigation: Weigh a piece of steel wool, rinse it with water, push the steel wool into the bottom of a test tube, invert the test tube in a beaker containing water, and adjust the water levels inside and outside the test tube until they are equal.

Over the next several days, students spent a few minutes of class time looking for and noting changes in this system. The most obvious changes were that the steel wool underwent a color change (as a result of rusting) and that the water level inside the test tube went up (as a result of removal of oxygen from the air). After a couple of days, the students were encouraged to propose hypotheses concerning the cause of these changes and then to design simple experimental variations to test these hypotheses. Many students speculated that rusting was somehow involved in the process; however, Mr. Criswell never confirmed this proposed explanation.

The underlying connection between the set of investigations was not clear to students at this point, but Mr. Criswell had laid the groundwork for both multiple explanations and resolution of the conflict. The initial discussion, demonstrations, and investigation involving rusting set up a pattern of introducing multiple threads of activity that were simultaneous and interconnected. These activity threads had different life spans, with some investigations taking a few moments and others being revisited multiple times over several weeks. Students were asked to continually revisit the models available to them, including their own model for combustion.

Simultaneous to their investigation of rusting, students were introduced to one of the fundamental questions facing chemistry in the 18th century: What happens to mass during a chemical change? Working in pairs, students were given three investigations in which they produced a chemical change and were asked to compare the masses before and after this change had occurred.

The first reaction involved the burning of steel wool: iron + oxygen → iron (III) oxide (rust). The second resulted in the formation of a precipitate, as well as the subsequent production of a gas: copper (II) chloride + sodium carbonate → copper (II) carbonate + sodium chloride. The third led to the release of gas: citric acid + sodium bicarbonate → sodium citrate + carbonic acid → sodium citrate + carbon dioxide + water.

All three of the reactions were designed to produce data that initially seemed to contradict Lavoisier's law of conservation of mass, because they did not take into account a gas as either one of the reactants (in the first case) or a product (in the second and third cases).

After the students shared their results with each other, Mr. Criswell presented Lavoisier's law. He noted that this law has been generally accepted (with some caveats) since Lavoisier introduced it in the late 1700s.

MR. CRISWELL: So can we try and summarize what happened to the masses in all three of the investigations?

KEVIN: Well, sometimes mass went up, sometimes it went down, and sometimes it stayed the same, so it's not the same every time for every reaction.

MR. CRISWELL: But we have the law of conservation of mass from Lavoisier that says that should not happen, so what is going on with our data?

EMILY: Well, in ours we could see a gas bubbling off, so maybe the mass went down for us because we lost some with the gas.

MR. CRISWELL: OK, so that is a possible explanation for why the mass went down, but what would make it go up? Group that did the burning steel wool, yours went up, right?

ROSH: Yes, but we are not sure why exactly.

The class's data did not support the conclusion that mass is conserved. "What can account for this discrepancy?" Mr. Criswell asked. Students were then presented the challenge of redesigning their experiments to take these gases into account. This proposition is simple in the case of the reaction involving a precipitate and the one involving the production of a gas. The burning of the steel wool is problematic, however, particularly because the result obtained is counterintuitive—the mass actually shows an *increase*. The following day Mr. Criswell brought the investigation with steel wool into the conversation about conservation of mass:

MR. CRISWELL:  You have been looking for changes in the test tubes for the last couple days. What have you observed?

EMILY:  The water in the tube went up.

ROSH:  And the steel wool rusted.

MR. CRISWELL:  How do you know it rusted?

KEVIN:  It turned brown and got all crusty, you can see it on the tube.

MR. CRISWELL:  What is rust? I mean what is going on chemically when something rusts?

KEVIN:  Oxidation.

MR. CRISWELL:  OK, fine, that is a nice science word, but what does it mean? Think about the different parts of the word.

EMILY:  It has something to do with oxygen.

ROSH:  It means combining with oxygen.

MR. CRISWELL:  Combining with oxygen? But where does the oxygen come from in the tube?

ROSH:  It comes from the water. There is oxygen in water.

EMILY:  No, it is in the air. The oxygen is in the air and when it combines with the steel wool it gets used up, and that makes a vacuum and the water gets sucked up into the tube.

Once the connection had been made and Mr. Criswell had clarified some of the points about air pressure and why the water level rose in the tube, the students were left on their own to consider the implications for both the water level change in the test tube (with the rusting steel wool) and the mass increase when the steel wool was burned.

# Synthesis

At this point in the curriculum, Mr. Criswell had a multitude of activity threads in the story of combustion open for students to consider and draw on. The students had encountered spontaneous human combustion, physical and chemical change, and conservation of mass. They had conducted investigations involving rusting steel wool, burning steel wool, precipitates, and the production of gases. Mr. Criswell had not attempted to resolve these threads into an overall pattern or model, yet the goal of this complexity was not confusion and lack of resolution. The goal was for students to remain perplexed (and thus engaged and inquiring) until they could bring all of this complexity to coherent synthesis—to combine all the empirical work they had done with conflicting explanations of the underlying phenomenon.

Resolution was provided not by Mr. Criswell directly, but by the students themselves as they brought evidence from their own empirical investigations to bear on the problem and deliver their own explanations of the ties between these investigations. This process of synthesis allowed students to connect their understandings about their investigations to the normative understandings of science. Students' developing explanations were facilitated and scaffolded by Mr. Criswell, who provided a rationale for creating explanations, connecting to everyday explanations, and assessing and providing feedback to students (McNeill and Krajcik, this volume, p. 123). The catalyst for students' synthesis in Mr. Criswell's class was a flawed model of combustion, the phlogiston theory.

The students had now completed a number of empirical investigations around the ideas of oxidation and combustion. At this point Mr. Criswell introduced students to phlogiston theory.

MR. CRISWELL: If we use the phlogiston theory as a model to describe what happens in your investigations, what does it tell us?

EMILY: As the chemical change happens, the reaction, some mass is lost because phlogiston escapes.

MR. CRISWELL: Is there any evidence you have that can't be explained using this theory?

ROSH: Well, yes, in ours the mass went up when we burned the steel wool. It should go down when it burns, because phlogiston is being released, right?

MR. CRISWELL: So how many of you are willing to accept phlogiston theory? [no students raise their hands] OK, but it is up to you to make an argument against it. Use the investigations and the data from the class, from both your group and your classmates, as you form your own explanation.

Mr. Criswell pointed out to students that the phlogistonists accounted for anomalous data of this nature by postulating that phlogiston could have negative mass. Phlogistonists' defense of their ideas led to a discussion of the ad hoc modification of many theories in the history of science in order to allow them to explain anomalous data. To provide additional data for the students to consider, Mr. Criswell began the next day with a new investigation: a study of the preparation and properties of an unknown gas. Students were told that the gas was produced from a combination of hydrogen peroxide and potassium permanganate. Students were also told that the discoverer of the gas, Joseph Priestly, was a supporter of the phlogiston theory until his death. Students were to undertake the preparation of the gas (oxygen) on their own and study the reactions of this gas with several materials (a glowing splint, a candle, charcoal, sulfur, steel wool, and magnesium ribbon).

Because students were already familiar with oxygen from previous lab work in class, they quickly identified the mystery gas. Again, Mr. Criswell did not confirm this conjecture, but pressed students to consider carefully the implications for the various investigations preceding the mystery gas investigation. Students were asked to use their identification to make predictions concerning the products of the various reactions they studied during the experiment. All of these built the empirical foundation for the development of their own scientific model of burning and for the summative activity.

A few days later students were asked to use the scientific model of combustion they had been developing to explain how a candle burns. Initially, they expected this would be a relatively easy undertaking—until they realized how difficult it was to isolate what was actually burning in the candle (the wax? the wick? something soaked into the wick?). Students soon found it necessary to design their own experiments to try to parse out the role of each of the parts of the candle.

Students were given two days to gather their data and observations and develop their explanation pertaining to the question of how a candle burns. During that time, Mr. Criswell acted as expert colleague and circulated around the room, pressing students on the interpretations they were making from the experiments being conducted.

MR. CRISWELL: I don't really see how your explanation is taking into account the mass increasing when the steel wool was burned. Can you tell me how that fits in?

KEVIN: Well, that data was from another group, so I didn't really think about it. I thought we just had to explain what our group found.

MR. CRISWELL: Sorry, you have to take everyone's data into account. And you also have to a make sure that when you say something like "for something to burn oxygen must be present," as you said here, that you give evidence from the experiments we did in class. You have to make sure you can back up your claims with evidence.

Mr. Criswell also reminded students that no knowledge claim could be included in their explanation that did not have empirical support from their own experimental results. With the last portion of the time allotted for this investigation, students were asked to synthesize their results into a formal report.

Student reports were collected and a grand debriefing session was held, in which all of the activity threads from the past weeks were brought together. Mr. Criswell presented a model of burning known as the Triangle of Fire (fuel, oxygen, and heat). Students discussed how this model explains the process of a candle burning. The scientific explanation (with the *wax* as the fuel) was presented and compared to the conclusions students reached. Viable rationales for reaching alternative conclusions were considered. Mr. Criswell focused students' attention on the validity of their logic, as opposed to achieving some predetermined correct answer.

The Triangle of Fire model was compared to phlogiston theory. Specifically, phlogiston theory can explain how a candle burns, but it cannot explain the result obtained in the oxygen preparation experiment (in which a candle burned in pure oxygen maintained its flame much longer than one burned in air). Finally, the scientific explanation of how a candle burns was used to propose an analogous scientific explanation of how human combustion can occur (known as the "wick effect"). Mr. Criswell concluded the discussion by showing the students the last part of the spontaneous human combustion video, which presents experimental evidence for the wick effect explanation.

# Conclusion

Mr. Criswell's classroom exemplifies three key elements of inquiry science pedagogy: perplexity, model testing, and synthesis. Students engaged in multiple activities over many weeks with activity threads from different investigations coming to resolution and then being revisited in the context of larger themes and patterns. The classroom community was asked to generate multiple explanations for individual investigations, as well as test models, that explain multiple phenomena, and all tests had to be grounded in students' own empirical investigations. Mr. Criswell did not dispense correct answers, and answers were not the primary goal of the students' work. The synthesis in which students were engaged had a clear set of criteria for choosing a model or theory. The model had to be empirically adequate, had to explain a range of phenomena, and could not be ad hoc. The only synthesis Mr. Criswell accepted from students was a thoughtful and empirically supported explanation that could encompass multiple, seemingly conflicting pieces of data from a number of different phenomena—exactly the goal of any scientific theory. By creating an environment of sustained yet evolving scientific perplexity, Mr. Criswell could support his students in doing the hard thinking—the supposing and critiquing. Although these students were not creating new knowledge for an external audience, they were engaged in scientific discovery, model testing, and theory building.

One of the most interesting things about this sequence of activities from Mr. Criswell's room was the degree to which it was both teacher directed *and* exemplary inquiry science pedagogy. Much of the literature on inquiry science argues explicitly, implicitly, or in the form of levels of inquiry (e.g., Schwab 1962) that student-directed inquiry is of a higher order or value than more teacher-directed versions. However, the example of Mr. Criswell's chemistry class shows that by careful, long-range planning a teacher can provide opportunities for students to engage in inquiry activities that provide greater insight into the history, content, and nature of science than a more open version of inquiry might. It is further evidence that we educators need to look beyond a single idealized version of classroom science inquiry and begin to understand the elements of inquiry pedagogy that make it a powerful instructional approach.

# Field Studies as a Pedagogical Approach to Inquiry

**Daniel P. Shepardson, Purdue University**
**Theodore J. Leuenberger, Benton Central Jr.-Sr. High School, Oxford, Indiana**

Field studies are a valuable way to engage students in scientific inquiry. They involve students in planning and conducting their own environmental investigations, allowing them to control their own learning experiences. Pedagogically, this process allows students to generate their own questions, create their own procedures for collecting evidence, and use data as the basis for their explanations. By designing and conducting their own field studies, students learn science in a meaningful context, apply scientific knowledge to local environmental issues, use resources within and around the school, and link classroom science to real-world issues (see Stapp, Wols, and Staukoub 1996, an excellent resource for teachers on planning and integrating field studies and community-based problem solving into the science curriculum). Students who are uninterested in school science because it is not useful or relevant to the real world can be drawn in and engaged, according to Howe (1991).

The first step in an environmental field study should be for students to conduct an environmental site survey. Students start by collecting background information about the local environment to develop an understanding of the conditions and context of the field study site. This step focuses their attention on the issues and conditions at the site itself. The outcome is a field study well-suited to the site and of local significance.

The TerraServer website (*http://terraserver.microsoft.com*) or a similar site (e.g., Google Earth, *http://earth.google.com*) can be used to display aerial photographs and topographic maps of the site, providing an overview of the land use patterns and landforms. Review of aerial photographs provides insight and clues to environmental problems to be investigated, familiarizes students with the environment, and may define the physical boundaries for the field study. This analysis also provides insight into where monitoring or data collection sites might be established.

The second step is to conduct an on-site survey. The on-site survey is a visual assessment of the environment, providing a closer look at the environmental conditions and potential environmental impacts within the site.

As students collect their field data, they organize and analyze these data, drawing interpretations about the patterns they observe. The field work gives meaning to *doing* science, as well as to the science concepts used to make sense of the world. As the students begin to interpret and analyze their results, scientific resources are used to assist in constructing explanations of the data. To complete the field study, students prepare an authentic product that summarizes the context of their work, goals, hypotheses, procedures, data, and interpretations and explanations. Thus, through field studies, students experience science teaching that promotes inquiry.

# Classroom Example: Field Study in a Stream Environment

The following example from Ted's seventh-grade general science course illustrates field studies as an effective, inquiry-based pedagogical technique and culminates with students conducting their own field investigation. The example is designed to follow the integrated Indiana Science Standards.

Ted's class was composed of Caucasian (95%) and Hispanic (5%) students; 48% were girls and 52% were boys. The students came from a wide variety of social and economic backgrounds. The school district draws from a large rural area of mostly agricultural land. Most of the population is employed in nearby Lafayette, Indiana, the site of several industries as well as Purdue University. The science classroom was well equipped with the materials and supplies necessary to conduct inquiry activities. During the activities described here, Ted used several visuals with the students, including posters on water quality, stream ecology, and land use.

First, Ted introduced students to water monitoring techniques, including the physical, biological, and chemical properties of stream environments. Students then learned about water quality issues using an interactive CD, which defined the different water quality parameters and prepared students in the water testing procedures used in the Green Kit (an inexpensive stream monitoring kit available from a number of educational suppliers).

Next, students engaged in a watershed simulation to practice using the testing equipment and to learn how environmental factors and land use practices might affect stream environments. During the simulation, students conducted the water quality tests at four different locations within a hypothetical watershed. Students used the results of the tests to explain how land use practices in the watershed affected the stream environment.

The watershed simulation prepared students to test for nitrates, phosphates, dissolved oxygen, pH, turbidity, temperature, and *E. coli*. Macroinvertebrates were also introduced as biological indicators. Macroinvertebrates are large (macro) organisms that lack a backbone (invertebrate) and may be seen with the naked eye. Students viewed macroinvertebrate cards for each site and identified the type and number of each macroinvertebrate at that site. Based on this biological data students drew conclusions about water quality at each site. Ted showed the students preserved macroinvertebrate samples to help them recognize the macroinvertebrates they might observe during their stream investigations. These experiences provided students with the foundation for building a conceptual model of stream environments (Figure 5.1).

After reviewing the testing techniques and possible environmental factors and land use practices that might affect stream environments, Ted presented students with a site survey of the field study area. An on-site survey would be best, but due to time and transportation limitations, in this case an in-class survey was conducted. Ted showed students an aerial photograph and topographic map of the field study area obtained from the TerraServer website. Within the field study area are found a major stream (Little Pine Creek) that drains farmland and forested areas, with a small, rural community on its banks about five miles upstream; a small tributary (Sugar Run), which begins in a cow pasture and flows through a forested area before entering Little Pine Creek; and a human-made pond, fed primarily by Sugar Run. The students viewed photographs of these areas so that they could get an idea of

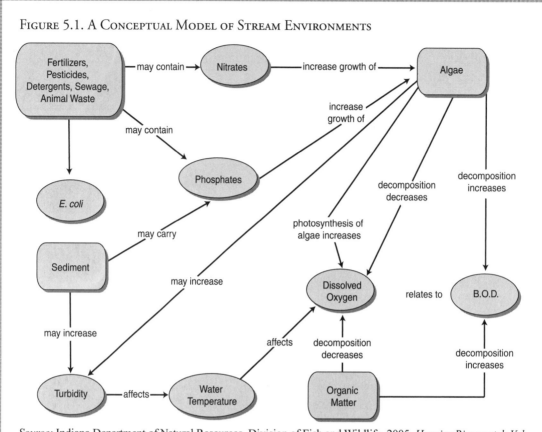

FIGURE 5.1. A CONCEPTUAL MODEL OF STREAM ENVIRONMENTS

*Source:* Indiana Department of Natural Resources, Division of Fish and Wildlife. 2005. *Hoosier Riverwatch Volunteer Stream Monitoring Training Manual*, p. 33. Hoosier Riverwatch website: *www.in.gov/dnr/riverwatch*.

the environmental factors and local land use practices that might influence this stream environment. In essence, students took a virtual field trip of the study site.

Students used the information and ideas from the site survey and the previous activities to develop a tentative mental model about stream environments and stream quality from which they identified and refined a guiding question. The question identified the dependent and independent variables of their stream investigation. For example, one question was, "How does the movement of water affect the dissolved oxygen in the water?" Students identified the movement of water as being the independent factor and the dissolved oxygen as being the dependent factor. Using these factors, the class developed a hypotheses—for example, "If the water is moving, then the dissolved oxygen will be higher." Students then planned an investigation to gather data pertinent to the hypothesis. During the site survey, the students identified two areas of Little Pine Creek that were different. One location showed water moving rapidly over rocks and another showed that water had been trapped in a small stagnant pool.

All students gathered authentic data pertinent to their individual investigations at the site. Later, in the classroom, students presented that data as graphs or charts (types of models) as evidence to support their explanations. Students developed their explanations based on the data, and these were then discussed by the class, where alternative explanations could be presented. This type of classroom conversation generates an authentic argument (see Chapter 1). The presentation and discussion of the individual student investigations gave the class a holistic view of the Little Pine Creek watershed.

Based on their experiences, the students constructed tentative mental models about stream environments. For example, as represented in Figure 5.2, students saw that the amount of dissolved oxygen in the water was affected by the physical and biological parameters of the stream. In this case, riffles add oxygen to the water and cooler water holds more oxygen; algae, through

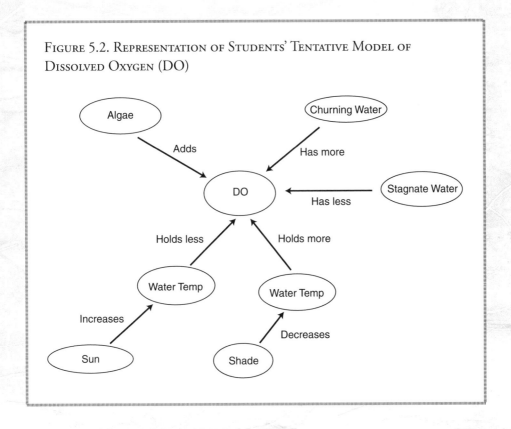

FIGURE 5.2. REPRESENTATION OF STUDENTS' TENTATIVE MODEL OF DISSOLVED OXYGEN (DO)

photosynthesis, add oxygen to the water. The quality or health of the stream environment was determined by the level of dissolved oxygen. Higher levels of dissolved oxygen support different types of macroinvertebrates (e.g., stonefly and mayfly nymphs); therefore, the stream is healthier.

## Teacher Reflection

The highlight for me (Ted) was the variety of interactions that took place among students and with me as they worked through each step of the process. Initially, each question had to be refined, each hypothesis developed, and each investigation transformed into a test of the hypothesis. Some students didn't quite get it the first time. A pair of students presented as their problem, "How will dissolved oxygen affect the temperature of the water?" Here they had included two water quality parameters and no environmental factors. With these students, I discussed the environmental factors that could affect those water quality factors. I helped them see that dissolved oxygen was not an environmental factor that might affect temperature. They amended their question to, "How will shade affect the temperature of the water?" Requiring students to present their ideas provides the teacher with an opportunity to help students develop good thinking strategies and to refine their tentative mental models.

Especially satisfying were the conversations that occurred in the field as students worked with the tests and the investigation site to collect their data. Students were excited about getting outside into the real environment. The physical presence of the testing site either confirmed or altered student ideas. For example, a pair of students had planned to take an *E. coli* sample in Little Pine Creek above and below the mouth of Sugar Run, thinking that the cow pasture at the head of Sugar Run might change the *E. coli* levels in Little Pine Creek. They noticed that the amount of water exiting Sugar Run was very small and realized that perhaps there was not enough water being introduced from Sugar Run into Little Pine Creek to make a difference. After discussing the problem, they decided to test the water in Sugar Run before it entered Little Pine Creek. By making this change, they collected more meaningful data. Some students doubted their original data and asked to collect additional data to confirm or correct their findings. Many learning experiences are available in the field that cannot be duplicated in the classroom.

In the final stage of the activity, students presented their findings and defended their explanations to the class. In one case, a student had hypothesized that dissolved oxygen would be lower in the still water of the pond than in the ripples of the creek. After taking two sets of data, she found opposite results and had trouble explaining why. Another student observed that the pond water looked greenish and thought perhaps the algae within the water caused the difference, explaining that photosynthesis would contribute oxygen to the pond. Throughout the presentation and discussion of results students gained a deeper understanding of the scientific process and of the biological, chemical, and physical aspects of stream environments. Although students constructed their own understanding, this personal meaning was not constructed in isolation from other students (as suggested by Bishop 1985; Rogoff 1990). I have found that students respond well to appropriate inquiry challenges like the one outlined in this chapter.

## Student Reflections

Students overwhelmingly enjoyed doing their field study. A number of students believed that doing the field study matched their learning styles: "I think I learn more doing hands-on learning," one student said. Conducting the water quality tests in the field made the tests more meaningful. As another student said, "It really helped me learn, because we were actually outside doing the tests ourselves. That is when I finally, completely figured out what my teacher was talking about."

The field study also helped students develop an understanding about how to design and conduct an investigation. Planning the investigation helped students learn to write a hypothesis that clearly stated the independent and dependent variables. Many of the students noted that the importance of the experience was its connection to the real world. One said, "In the long run it will help us not only in the classroom but in real life." The experience helped students see the real connection between land use practice and stream quality. It allowed the students to determine if land use practices were impacting Sugar Run, as several students noted: "It showed me if cow pastures would affect the pH in Sugar Run or not" and that "a cow pasture by Sugar Run puts more *E. coli* into the stream."

Most students thought that developing their own question and investigation was best. Statements by students included the following: "I would rather come up with my own question because it lets you choose what you are going to do and how you are going to do it." "It challenged me to find answers." "I would rather make my own up. This is because you get to learn what you want to learn not [what] the teacher [wants you to learn]." This gave students ownership and responsibility in their learning. "If I'm given the question and the investigation, it's like I'm not doing the work," one student said.

A few students, however, wanted the teacher to provide the question, as exemplified by the following student statements: "I would rather be given the question and investigation, because it would be less confusing and easier." "I think we should be given a question because we can pick something really easy, and I think we need to be challenged more."

## Science Educator Reflection

I (Dan) see the interactive CD and watershed simulation as guided inquiry activities, what Windschitl (in Chapter 1) calls *supporting activities*. These activities provided the students with the experiences and knowledge to develop the tentative mental models they needed in order to plan and conduct the water quality tests and organize their information, data, and experiences about the Little Pine Creek watershed. This process is adaptive in that students organize the experiential world based on their tentative mental models (as described by Lerman 1989).

These experiences required students to physically and mentally act on phenomena (as in Piaget 1970) and to interact with members of the community (as in Vygotsky 1962/1986)—other students and the teacher—in order to construct personal meaning (as in Driver and Bell 1986). For example, students physically performed the water quality tests and used their tentative mental models to think and talk about these tests within the context of the environmental factors and land use practices surrounding Little Pine Creek.

The students' stream investigations not only reflected open inquiry (i.e., they were more learner directed), but reflected what scientists do in the real world to investigate and monitor stream environments. In essence, these students were modeling the scientific process. Windschitl (see Chapter 1) refers to this type of experience as core knowledge-building activities. This is not to say that the teacher takes a hands-off approach but rather, as this teacher did, assists students as needed, providing the type and amount of structure based on individual student needs. For example, Ted provided some students with more guidance than others in developing and framing their questions, and stating their hypotheses. Had he not done so, those students would have floundered in doing the inquiry and learning the science.

Poor inquiries often lead to scientifically inappropriate or meaningless understandings. In essence, these students identified their own questions and designed their own investigations. The students used appropriate tools to collect their data; they then interpreted their data and used scientific knowledge to explain their results, using data as evidence. They communicated their procedures, data, and explanations to others, creating opportunities for argumentation and the presentation of alternative explanations.

Finally, students were learning about macroinvertebrates as biological indicators of stream quality. Biological monitoring is the study of living organisms for the purpose of determining environmental conditions. In this particular classroom, students were conducting a biosurvey—the identification and quantification of macroinvertebrates. Macroinvertebrates are good indicators of stream quality because they are affected by the physical and chemical conditions of the stream, are unable to move away from pollutants or events that impact the stream, show the cumulative or synergistic effects of pollutants, and vary in their tolerance to pollution. The quality of the stream is determined by the presence and abundance of different macroinvertebrates, using a model that categorizes the macroinvertebrates based on their sensitivity or tolerance to pollution and that results in a numerical rating of the stream. Different types of streams (e.g., rocky bottom, muddy bottom) and different states require the use of different rating systems.

In this way students were addressing the National Science Education Standards (NSES) (NRC 1996) life science standards about populations and ecosystems. Students were learning that the type and number of organisms (i.e., species richness and abundance) found in an ecosystem are dependent on the abiotic factors of that system—in this case, the chemical and physical conditions of the stream. For example, the presence and abundance of stonefly and mayfly nymphs will decline as the level of dissolved oxygen decreases.

# Other Field Studies: Invasive Species and Air Quality

Although this classroom example illustrated field studies–based pedagogy through stream investigations, there are numerous biological concepts that may be learned through field studies. Students could conduct field studies to investigate the distribution or ecological impact of invasive species (such as garlic mustard or bush honeysuckle on woodland environments). In such field studies, students could compare the abiotic and biotic characteristics of field plots containing invasive species to plots without invasive species. Such comparisons would lead to data-based discussions about biodiversity, species interactions, and competition for resources such as abiotic factors (e.g., light, water, and temperature), differences in biological adaptations, and perhaps the extinction of indigenous species because of their inability to compete with invasive species for resources—all of which topics are aligned with the life science standards for Populations and Ecosystems and Diversity and Adaptations of Organisms (NRC 1996, pp. 157–158).

Students could conduct field studies investigating air quality using lichens as biological indicators. Foliose (leafy) and fruticose (shrubby) lichens tend to be found in areas with clean air, while crustose (crusty) lichens can survive in areas of poor air quality. A number of websites describe the use of lichens as biological indicators; a general air quality index is as follows (from polluted to clean air): no lichens, grey-green crusty lichens, orange crusty lichens, leafy lichens, shrubby lichens (Frank, Luera, and Stapp 1996). It is also important to consider the size of the lichens; in general, the larger the lichens the better the air quality. In essence, students identify sampling sites on trees from different field sites and compare the type and quantity of lichens (see Frank, Luera, and Stapp 1996 for a detailed protocol). This leads to data-driven discussions about air quality and environmental degradation, which aligns with the standards for Science in Personal and Social Perspectives (NRC 1996, pp. 166–170, 193–199).

As shown in the classroom examples and in these examples, field studies provide teachers and students with unique opportunities to investigate their local environments in authentic ways. Field studies are data-driven experiences, are extended over time, and use evidence to develop and support explanations. Field studies provide the opportunity for students to learn science and develop inquiry abilities in a meaningful context—the students' real world.

# Conclusion

This chapter described guided inquiry activities used as a means to build students' knowledge structures or tentative mental models, providing the experience necessary to be successful in their stream investigations. The stream investigations built from students' tentative mental models to identifying guiding questions. Students defined their own learning by designing an investigation and collecting data to answer their questions and test their tentative mental models. In this way the inquiries were data driven, and the data became central to learning; that is, students formulated explanations based on the data and used scientific ideas to explain the data. These students shared their investigations, data, and explanations with others, supporting science-specific forms of talk (see Chapter 1). The teacher assisted students as needed to ensure that they developed their inquiry abilities and learned science.

The teacher engaged students in the fundamental abilities to do scientific inquiry as outlined by the National Research Council (1996, 2000). This teacher, like many, spent less time addressing the fundamental understandings about scientific inquiry. For example, the notion that different kinds of questions require different kinds of investigations or that technology enhances the accuracy of data collection was not explicitly addressed. This experience did implicitly expose students to the notions that scientific knowledge guides scientific investigations and that scientific explanations emphasize evidence.

# Creating Coherent Inquiry Projects to Support Student Cognition and Collaboration in Physics

**6**

**Douglas B. Clark, Arizona State University**
**S. Raj Chaudhury, Christopher Newport University**

As a physics teacher, you have computer programs, labs, and engaging activities for your students. Individually, these excellent tools allow your students to investigate fascinating aspects of the physics curriculum. Integrating them into coherent inquiry projects, however, can dramatically increase their potential to support students' cognition and collaboration around core physics concepts.

The inquiry template presented in this chapter incorporates the four conversations outlined in Chapter 1, with an additional focus on engaging students in sharing and critiquing one another's reasoning as they collaboratively refine their understandings of physics phenomena. The template involves three phases: (1) students observe and reflect on phenomena and make predictions about underlying mechanisms, (2) students gather data to investigate these mechanisms as they build and refine their models, and (3) students discuss, critique, and refine these models within a larger group.

As discussed in Chapter 1, these phases occur in iterative cycles rather than a strictly linear sequence. These phases provide, however, a useful general trajectory for inquiry. Certainly, this template is not the only inquiry approach for physics. There are many valuable approaches depending on your pedagogical goals, but this one has the advantage of flexibly combining hands-on labs, simulations, discussions, and other activities into coherent inquiry projects across the curriculum.

In the following sections, the phases of the template will be discussed and illustrated with examples from a National Science Foundation–funded project called "Probing Your Surroundings." Thermal equilibrium (or steady state temperature) is a challenging concept connected to many other core thermodynamics concepts, as well as several alternative conceptions grounded in students' everyday experiences. Most scientists agree that all objects in a constant-temperature room should become the same temperature over time unless they produce their own heat (e.g., a lighted lightbulb or a living person). This happens because of a net heat transfer between higher temperature objects and lower temperature objects until all of the objects (including the air) are the same temperature.

Students, however, are aware from their daily experiences that some materials often feel hotter or colder than others in the room. Metal objects, for example, generally feel colder than wooden objects. The metal objects feel colder because they have a greater coefficient of thermal conductivity, which essentially means that heat transfers more quickly through them. As a result, heat transfers more quickly out of a person's hand (which is a higher temperature) and into a metal chair than it does into a wooden table of the same temperature. Hence, even though the metal chair and wooden table are the same temperature as each other and the rest of the room, the metal chair feels colder because of its higher thermal conductivity.

Students often connect this experiential knowledge about how objects feel to their estimation of the temperature of those objects. Students may believe that metal objects are hotter or colder than wood objects in the same environment because that's the way they feel. For example, metal objects in a warm oven feel hotter than other objects, so students assume that objects do not eventually reach the same temperature. To support this assumption, students often selectively revise other school-instructed thermodynamics ideas connected to thermal equilibrium, such as thermal conductivity. Students may assume that metals are hotter because they are better conductors and they "conduct in" more heat. In order for students to build robust understandings of science, they must make sense of core concepts like thermal equilibrium.

# The Inquiry Template Phases

## Phase One: Observing, Reflecting, and Making Predictions About Underlying Mechanisms

From a constructivist perspective, students learn by building on their existing ideas. As part of this process, students benefit significantly from reflecting on what they know about the phenomena under investigation and predicting possible mechanisms.

Engaging students' interest and providing bridges to their everyday experiences support cognitive engagement. You can begin the thermal equilibrium inquiry by reading the following excerpt from a home-improvement website: "Plastic bathtubs are better than metal bathtubs because plastic is not as naturally cold a material as metal, so the hot water in your bath should stay hotter longer than it did in the metal bathtub."

After this example, point out that people talk about objects being "naturally hot" or "naturally cold" and ask students to think about what they mean. As part of this process, prompt students to write their initial ideas in a journal. Most students assume that metal objects in the room are colder than the other objects. Students may provide reasons such as "the metal attracts cold" or "wool is warmer because wool warms things up." The goal of this phase is to engage your students in active reflection upon their prior ideas and experiences to provide a foundation to guide their subsequent investigations, as well as to facilitate their re-examination and revision of these initial ideas during the project.

After engaging students' interest, you should prompt your students to predict the outcome of a measurement or to hypothesize about the causal mechanisms driving the phenomena. A measurement contrary to students' predictions has the advantage of potentially creating a moment of cognitive dissonance you can use to promote focused thinking about the phenomena.

Students often focus on the surface aspects of phenomena rather than on the aspects that experts would consider critical. Students also have difficulty generating detailed explanations of phenomena. You should provide supports for students during the prediction process to help them focus on the salient issues and features. Hints, specific question prompts, and other scaffolding can work wonders. Furthermore, these supports help students articulate their models in enough detail so that other students notice differences and want to discuss these differences in the third phase of the template.

Toward this goal, ask students to create an initial "principle" to explain the temperatures of the various objects in the room. Table 6.1 shows some phrases students can use to create their principles. You may provide these lists of phrases on a worksheet or use flashcards or other media. Students can use these phrases to create principles such as the following:

- When placed in the same room for 24 hours, all objects become the same temperature as the room unless they produce their own heat energy. These objects feel different because they transfer heat at different rates. (Note: Scientifically correct version.)

- When placed in the same room for 24 hours, objects that are good insulators stay at their original temperature regardless of the temperature of the room unless air can get inside them. These objects feel different because they are different temperatures. (Note: Materials with low thermal conductivity, such as wool and wood, often confuse students because such materials never feel as hot or cold as metal or glass in the same environment. Students assume that these "insulators" don't change temperature.)

Where possible, physics inquiry projects should be situated within a real-world context with potential for connection to students' interests. For instance, high school students about to get their driver's licenses generally find a lesson on the role of air bags in car crashes to be practical and motivating. You will be helping them understand one-dimensional acceleration (and deceleration). Have students focus on the salient issues and levels of abstraction during their construction of their predicted model. You might also consider explicit instruction or discussion about the role of causal mechanisms in scientific inquiry to help students understand the goals of the lesson as well as the nature of science.

# Phase Two: Gathering Data to Investigate the Mechanisms and Build and Refine a Model

Although *gedanken experiments* (thought experiments) play a critical role in physics when laboratory measurements cannot keep pace with theoretical

TABLE 6.1. OPENING SENTENCE PROMPT AND SUGGESTED PHRASES STUDENTS CAN USE TO BUILD THEIR EXPLANATORY PRINCIPLES

Choose one phrase from each column below to complete the following statement and build an explanatory principle: **When placed in the same room for 24 hours...**

| 1. What kinds of objects? | 2. What happens to the objects? | 3. Qualifiers or conditions? | 4. How do the objects feel and why? |
|---|---|---|---|
| • All objects<br><br>• Some objects<br><br>• Hot objects<br><br>• Metal and glass objects<br><br>• Wood objects<br><br>• Cold objects<br><br>• Objects that are good conductors<br><br>• Objects that are good insulators | • stay at their original temperature regardless of the temperature of the room<br><br>• become the same temperature as each other but not the room<br><br>• become close to but not exactly the same temperature as each other<br><br>• become the same temperature as the room<br><br>• become close to but not exactly the same temperature as the room<br><br>• are at a different temperature than other objects in the same room | • even if they produce their own heat energy.<br><br>• unless they produce their own heat energy.<br><br>• because they are made of different materials.<br><br>• unless air can get inside them.<br><br>• but only on their surface, not inside them. | • The objects feel the same as each other because they are the same temperature.<br><br>• The objects feel different because they are different temperatures.<br><br>• The objects feel different because they transfer heat at different rates.<br><br>• The objects feel different because they transfer heat at the same rate.<br><br>• The objects feel the same because they transfer heat at the same rate. |

advances, physics teachers have powerful tools and simulations to support their students' investigations. Donovan and Bransford (2005), however, raise a cautionary note in *How Students Learn: Science in the Classroom*:

> *Even when science instruction is shifted in the direction of engaging in scientific inquiry (as is happening more frequently in today's*

*classrooms), it can be easy to emphasize giving students "recipes for experiments." ... These lockstep approaches shortchange observation, imagination and reasoning.* (pp. 403–405)

You should focus and organize data gathering to help students build initial models to support their predictions and later refine those models in the face of further evidence or peer critique.

The inquiry goals are the same whether you use traditional laboratory equipment (e.g., thermometers, beakers, stopwatches, and other standard labware), computer-based probeware or micro-computer-based probeware (CBLs or MBLs), or computational models (simulations), but you should carefully consider the different data-gathering logistics for each of these approaches. Each approach has strengths and weaknesses in terms of your overall inquiry goals for integrating data gathering with model building and investigation (Bell 2005; Millar 2004). Traditional labware offers the benefit that students are often familiar with consumer versions of certain objects (e.g., thermometers). At the same time, labware requires careful training to ensure data quality (e.g., gauging the meniscus level on a column of water in a graduated cylinder). On the other hand, the use of computer-based probeware reduces the data-recording burden and facilitates multiple trials, which encourages further experimentation, a necessary step that allows students to revisit their initial experimental parameters in the process of building and refining their models.

Often, however, the phenomena under investigation will involve sizes or timescales too small or too large to measure in the laboratory. Students cannot, for example, measure the average kinetic energy of gas molecules in a heated container at the molecular level with the labware and probeware typically available in secondary classrooms. Simulations (computational models) provide an invaluable addition to your tool chest in this regard. Simulations also have the advantage of allowing investigation of systems that would pose safety hazards in the classroom (e.g., radioactive decay or boiling water). Students working in pairs at a computer can collaboratively run simulations using initial parameters, observe the outcomes, record those outcomes, change variables in the simulation, record the new outcomes, and refine their models. You may need to help students connect their models and real-world observations. Students encounter difficulties investigating thermodynamics, for example, because "we neither see nor measure heat transfer *directly*. The quantities that we observe are masses and temperature changes, and we *infer* the amount of heat transferred from these observations" (Aarons 1990, p. 20).

In the second phase of the thermal equilibrium inquiry, students collect real-time data about the temperatures of objects found inside the classroom and explore interactive simulations dealing with such ideas as heat transfer, thermal conductivity, and thermal sensation. As students work through the activities, they record the data they gather and describe their observations. Together, these activities provide students with the empirical data and other scientific ideas needed to stimulate productive argumentation during the third phase.

You may give students thermometers, temperature strips (available at pet stores), or probeware (or a combination of the three) with which to make their measurements. Sometimes pedagogy dictates the most appropriate choice, as illustrated in the following vignette:

Mr. Caton's physical science students had completed their predictions and were ready to take measurements to test them. Mr. Caton knew that his middle school students often interpreted differences as small as a few tenths of a degree (e.g., between his lunch apple sitting on his desk and a metal chair leg) to mean that all objects did not eventually reach thermal equilibrium. So he decided to issue "low-tech" temperature strips (with a sensitivity of about one degree) as opposed to ultra-sensitive electronic probes, which measure one-tenth of a degree variations. Two days later, Mr. Caton presented a whole-class demonstration, in which he melted chocolate chips at the end of a long metal rod. Mr. Caton decided that the rapid rate of heat conduction in the metal rod called for the speed and precision of probeware. As the demonstration ran, students could observe the visual (and aromatic) chocolate melting process and the real-time graphing display from the temperature probe simultaneously. Not only could Mr. Caton discuss the connections between his demonstration and a similar computer simulation from the students' project, but he could initiate discussions about precision in terms of the temperature strips and the probeware.

Cognitive science research indicates that people learn best when actively engaged in knowledge-centered, learner-centered, assessment-centered activities (Bransford, Brown, and Cocking 2000). These three attributes don't necessarily spontaneously accompany one another. Knowledge-centered activities, for example, don't ensure learner-centered activities. Mr. Caton could have achieved a knowledge-centered approach by simply providing his students with a table of thermal conductivity coefficients and a worksheet to compare heat conduction in iron and wood. Mr. Caton's inquiry approach, however, made the activity more learner-centered by allowing students to discover the differences for themselves and asking further questions like, "Do all metals conduct heat at the same rate?"

This knowledge-centered *and* learner-centered approach allows students to engage with some of *their* questions as opposed to strictly following the teacher's directions. Finally, Mr. Caton provided students with formative and summative feedback that focused not only on the facts but also on the core ideas, connections, and processes of the project so that his assessments appropriately reflected, aligned with, and supported the rest of the activities within the curriculum.

## Phase Three: Critiquing and Arguing Models Within a Larger Group

During the third phase, students examine different perspectives with the purpose of reaching agreement on acceptable claims or courses of action. The goal should focus on solving problems to advance knowledge rather than "winning" or "losing." Your students should use each others' ideas to negotiate and construct a shared understanding of the phenomenon under investigation in light of past experiences and new information.

To complete the third phase of the example thermal equilibrium inquiry, sort students into groups based on the revised principle they created during the second phase. The discussion groups should include students who have created different models so they can discuss multiple perspectives (i.e., their individual models). The members of a discussion group may enter an online threaded discussion forum or a face-to-face discussion with their principles included as the starting comments. Incorporating your students' own principles as the initial comments increases the social relevance and interest of the activity. The sorting process can be conducted by you, by software, or potentially by the students themselves (e.g., "Find three students who created different principles than you did.").

Figures 6.1–6.3 show transcripts of online discussions in a standard threaded discussion forum format (i.e., with the comments indented and placed beneath the parent comments to which they reply). The discussion segments (from data gathered in the Probing Your Surroundings project) include the original spelling and syntax from the actual discussions. Each discussion segment involves a different discussion group with different students. Students often require significant support to achieve high quality interactions, but these segments demonstrate the positive potential of student discussions in this phase.

In Figure 6.1, for example, three student pairs focus their attention on challenging the grounds of one another's claims. The students are not the only people who have an active role to play. You might encourage the students in this example to think about differences between closed systems and systems that have sinks and sources.

Whereas the students in the discussion in Figure 6.1 focused on the grounds of the comments, the students in the discussion in Figure 6.2 focused their challenges on interpretations of the phenomenon.

Finally, in the discussion segment in Figure 6.3, Pair A questions the experimental methods used by Pair B to gather evidence. Their query reflects a value judgment about what should count as valid data and what methods can satisfactorily generate such data. These types of questions are essential in the process of knowledge co-construction.

The students also raise an interesting question about Styrofoam. Styrofoam is well-known as an excellent insulator—both hot and cold drinks maintain their temperature longer when placed in cups made of this material. However, as both Pair A and B noted, there is nothing special about the temperature of the Styrofoam cup. The students' own questions, therefore, open up the door for connections to other portions of the physics curriculum.

All of these issues provide you with excellent opportunities to extend students' inquiry as a facilitator and coach during the discussion and after. As part of this process, you should have the students reflect back to the original problem and make final revisions to their model at the end of the third phase of inquiry. After students complete their final revisions, you should engage them in a larger discussion. In the thermal equilibrium inquiry example, you might have the students feel a metal chair leg and a wood desktop and then ask them, "Are the leg and the desktop the same temperature?" The ensuing discussion will give you an opportunity to help students reflect on their conceptual starting point and evaluate what they have learned.

You can use any generic online threaded forum for these discussions. Simply have the students "paste" or type their refined principles from the second phase

## Figure 6.1. Online Discussion Segment 1*

**Pair A** *(initial statement made by a student pair)*
Sometimes some objects in the same surroundings at room temperature become within a few degrees of the same temperature unless an object produces its own heat energy. At this point, the objects are within a few degrees even though they may feel different.

**Pair B** *(response to Pair A)*
grant a computer produces heat energy, and when you checked its tempature it was about the same as the others.

**Pair A** *(response to Pair B)*
A computer does produce heat energy, but that does not mean that the heat energy will travel into the outside plastic casing. Also computers do not produce enough heat energy to make a notable change. A computer has a fan inside it for the purpose of cooling it down, so it will cool down the computer and when you test the temperature it will not be higher than its surroundings.

**Pair B** *(response to Pair A)*
Mr. Jones said that it did.

**Pair C** *(response to Pair B)*
I think that you are a little off on your information. I don't think the chair and computers are the same temperature. It is obvious from my experiment with Brian that the chair leg was definetly cooler than the computor because the chair leg is metal and it produces it's own heat energy and the keyboard gets warmed from the wamrth of the electicity and my hand.

**Pair A** *(response to Pair C)*
Metal does not produce its own heat energy. If it did it would be different from room temperature. From my experiment, the metal chair leg was 23.2°C, which was almost exactly the room temperature. However, the comp might be warmer because it produces heat energy.

*Original spelling and syntax have been maintained.

Figure 6.2. Online Discussion Segment 2*

**Pair A** *(initial statement made by a student pair)*
In some situations all objects in the same surround at room temperature become within a few degrees of the same temperature even if an object produces its own heat energy. At this point, the objects are the same temperature even though they may feel different.

**Pair B** *(response to Pair A)*
If an object produces its own heat energy then it would not be the same temperature as other objects that dont produce heat energy. For example, when a light bulb is on it produces heat energy and is much hotter than other objects in the same suroundings. How do you explain this??????

**Pair C** *(response to Pair B)*
I agree with you, [Pair A], you are wrong!!!!

**Pair D** *(response to Pair C)*
I disagree with you. I agree with [Pair A].

**Pair C** *(response to Pair D)*
An object that produces heat will stay hoter than an object that does not produce heat. Like A LIGHT BULB, if it is on in a room it will be hoter than a table in the same room.

into the discussions as their starting comments. Online threaded discussion forums provide an optimal context for the ensuing discussions because (a) students have time to reflect on and revise their contributions before they submit them, and (b) these forums allow everyone to participate simultaneously rather than forcing students to compete with one another for a chance to speak. These forums can potentially facilitate more equitable participation than generally occurs in face-to-face settings.

If you do not have access to online discussion forums, discussions can be conducted in face-to-face groups. In this case, you might choose to have students use white boards or large pieces of paper to record or diagram the critiques of

## Figure 6.3. Online Discussion Segment 3*

**Pair A** *(initial statement made by a student pair)*
In some situations some objects in the same surroundings at room temperature become within a few degrees of the same temperature, but this is only on the surface of the objects, not inside them. At this point, the objects are within a few degrees even though they may feel different.

> **Pair B** *(response to Pair A)*
> What about a styrofoam cup? I took the temperature on the inside, and on the outside and it was the same.

> > **Pair A** *(response to Pair B)*
> > How would you take the temperature of the inside? Did you break it open or did you just put the temperature probe inside of the cup?

> > > **Pair B** *(response to Pair A)*
> > > I actually pushed the end of the probe into the styrofoam cup.

*Original spelling and syntax have been maintained.

each principle. Students can then move between the principles as they consider the evidence from the activity and other experiences.

Although students have previous everyday experience with arguments, you should provide specific instructions and supports for students to focus on use of evidence to support or challenge claims. A class discussion about how scientific argumentation differs from everyday argumentation in terms of the goals and what counts as evidence may also prove valuable (see Chapter 8). The statement "I disagree because the lab showed that the temperatures were the same" is more appropriate than "I disagree because he's wrong" or "I disagree because he's stupid." On a related note, students often accept presented information rather than question it. For this reason, you should guide students to question other students' principles and identify weaknesses in their arguments. Choosing topics for which students have ample access to evidence supports this process.

# Conclusion

As a physics teacher, you have an abundance of excellent resources to draw upon as you assemble your own projects. In traditional curricula, these resources and activities remain relatively unconnected—perhaps the students make predictions and gather data for one lab, use computers as part of another project, and occasionally engage in debate for nature of science or socioscientific topics. Although these activities have value individually, the template described in this chapter flexibly combines these resources and activities into coherent inquiry projects across the physics curriculum and provides much richer learning experiences for your students.

The basic formula is simple. In this template, students first observe and reflect on phenomena and make predictions about underlying mechanisms. Students then gather data to investigate these mechanisms as they build and refine their models. Finally, students discuss, critique, and refine these models within a larger group.

For the overall formula to succeed, however, you must carefully structure and guide each phase. The examples in this chapter highlight some specific issues for your consideration. Often you can integrate your current activities, labs, and computer programs into the three phases of the template through this approach. With careful planning and orchestration, you can create powerful pedagogical synergies to support students' cognition and collaboration around core physics concepts across the curriculum.

# Inquiry-Based Science Instruction for Students With Disabilities

7

**Kathy Cabe Trundle, Ohio State University**

Veronica is an outstanding science teacher, and I have enjoyed watching her for years. Each time I visit her class, I see the modifications she is using to help students learn and participate in science. As she is dedicated to having all students participate fully in class, she is always looking for new approaches that will make science even more accessible. During my last visit, she was having the students observe different single-celled eukaryotic organisms. As the students walked into the classroom, on their tables were traditional microscopes and laptops connected to digital microscopes and a variety of containers of water with different organisms. Beside each microscope were written directions and directions with pictures. Large pieces of paper and colored pencils were also laid out for students who wanted to draw their organism, and clay was available for those wanting to create a three-dimensional image.

As the students came into class, they quickly took their seats at their assigned tables. Veronica assigned each student to a team in order to maximize each student's learning opportunity. Once the students were settled, she explained that the activity would focus on just finding the organisms. Veronica challenged each group to find at least three different organisms. When they found an organism, they could draw it, create it out of clay, or take a digital picture with their microscope and post the picture on their laptop computer. Veronica kept the directions short, which let the students get started quickly.

As I watched the class, I found it difficult to identify the students with disabilities. All of the students were looking through the microscopes and finding organisms. Some of the students were using the regular microscopes, while other students had enlarged images on the computer screens. As students found organisms, they captured them digitally, drew them, or created clay sculptures. I was amazed at how detailed and intricate the drawings and sculptures made by the students with disabilities were. Veronica moved from group to group throughout the period, reinforcing the progress of students and demonstrating (as needed) how to use different techniques. It was an action-packed class that was over before I knew it.

As we work with increasing numbers of students with disabilities in our classrooms, Individual Education Plans, 504 Plans, and Intervention Plans are becoming more and more familiar terms in our professional vocabulary and more frequent realities to be considered as we plan our instruction. In science, these plans strive to include a wide range of students in our daily classroom activities. Including students with visual (low vision and blindness), hearing (limited hearing and deafness), mobility, emotional, and cognitive impairments in our development of classroom lessons ultimately makes the science class more inclusive. Moreover, it ensures that *all* students learn about science and become scientifically literate, which is a stated goal in the National Science Education Standards (NRC 1996).

Students with disabilities often are struggling readers who cannot successfully access and use print information. As a result, they usually experience difficulties with traditional science instruction, which typically relies on textbooks and other printed materials for instruction and assessment. Unfortunately, these difficulties can translate into a lack of performance in science class, as well as a lost opportunity to wonder about the natural world. Moving away from a reliance on reading to inquiry instruction affords students with disabilities an opportunity to access and think about the phenomena they encounter each day.

# Summary of the Research

## Traditional Instruction

When science instruction and assessments rely on reading and writing, students with disabilities are not as successful as their peers. This trend is evident in studies of classrooms and large-scale assessments. Donahoe and Zigmond (1988), for example, found that when science instruction and assessment were conventional, most of the students with disabilities were likely to earn a grade of D or below. In a science evaluation program for the state of New York, 69% to 75% of students without disabilities passed the test, while fewer than 50% of students with disabilities performed successfully (Cawley and Parmar 2001). A closer look at large-scale assessments reveals another problematic trend: Students with disabilities are likely to score even lower in science and mathematics than they do in reading, vocabulary, and writing (Harnisch and Wilkinson 1989). The lack of comparable scores can be attributed to students having to learn another language—that of science. Overall, traditional instruction can limit the success of students with disabilities in science class and in their academic careers.

# Inquiry-Based Instruction

The integration of inquiry into the science classroom provides an alternative approach for students with disabilities to learn scientific knowledge and skills. Moreover, this integration can contribute to building an inclusive classroom in which all children are valued, respected, and given the opportunity to fully participate in the class. In the classroom, inquiry-based instruction gives students with disabilities the opportunity to access information about science and to construct an understanding of the natural world. Research results indicate that inquiry-based science instruction benefits students' achievement, including students with learning disabilities (Mastropieri and Scruggs 1992; Scruggs, Mastropieri, and Boon 1998). For example, students who were taught using inquiry methods performed significantly better than those who were taught via a lecture method, and the inquiry method was significantly more effective for average- and low-ability students (Odubunmi and Balogun 1991). On performance-based assessments, students with learning disabilities who had been taught with inquiry-based instruction outperformed their typically developing peers (Bay et al. 1992).

Several studies report the benefits of inquiry-based science instruction for students who have a range of disabilities. Students with learning disabilities, mild mental retardation, autism (Mastropieri et al. 2001), visual impairments (Erwin, Ayala, and Perkins 2001), or hearing impairments or deafness (Borron 1978) were all able to successfully participate in an inquiry experience and explain their results. Moreover, as they engage in inquiry experiences, students with a wide range of disabilities are likely to become proficient in using science process skills, develop skills to work independently, and become motivated to learn science (Barman and Stockton 2002). An active environment for the students can result in better learning of concepts in science as well as students having more confidence in their own capabilities to participate in science (Dalton et al. 1997; Palincsar et al. 2001). Overall, a science-as-inquiry environment allows the greatest number of students to experience and learn about science.

# General Guidelines

Several strategies can be used to accommodate students with disabilities. One strategy is "universal design" (Null 1996; Rose and Meyer 2002)—that is, the modification of instruction and materials to ensure that all students can participate to the greatest extent possible. Universal design takes into consideration a wide range of individual characteristics for different people throughout their lifetimes, and it provides learning alternatives for students with differing abilities. Instructional methods that use a universal design include the following:

1. *Establishing an inclusive classroom setting that respects and values all diversity, including special physical and learning needs.* As a philosophy, universal design ensures that all students are valued in the classroom and that accommodations are made to ensure their learning.

2. *Providing physical, visual, and auditory access in the classroom, in laboratories, and during field experiences to ensure that all students have safe physical access to materials and experiences.* In the science classroom, physical accessibility can be accomplished by simple modifications, such as adjusting the height of a laboratory table to allow a student in a wheelchair to sit with peers or modifying laboratory equipment to make handling easier for students with limited manual dexterity.

3. *Using multiple modes for content access, including fieldwork, discussions, lectures, computer work, and inquiry experiences.* Simple modifications include summarizing print information orally prior to the lesson or activity, as well as providing the information to groups of students to discuss before the lesson. With these activities, students have access to the information in different formats.

4. *Creating and providing print materials in a simple format that students may access electronically through a website.* Prior to a science experiment, for example, a teacher can upload the directions for

the laboratory. The student can look at the directions prior to the experiment and prepare for the lesson accordingly.

5. *Encouraging students to interact with each other and their teachers through different formats such as e-mails or online discussion groups.* Online communications can allow students to communicate with one another without the pressure of giving an immediate response. Some students need more time and written comments as they process information. The online environment allows students to read the conversation and to reply in a time frame that is conducive to their processing of information.

6. *Providing feedback both during the learning experiences and after the assignment is complete.* Throughout a science lesson, the teacher should give ongoing feedback to students with disabilities. This ensures that students are provided with adequate directions and reinforcement to complete the activity.

7. *Allowing students to demonstrate their knowledge and understanding in varied ways, such as portfolios, presentations, and demonstrations, as well as on traditional tests and in written papers.* Creating concept maps and drawings and describing a science experience can also reveal students' knowledge and understanding. Concept maps, for example, can be used prior to an activity and afterwards to assess a student's growth in knowledge (Burgstahler 2004).

To accommodate students with disabilities during inquiry experiences, a teacher can do the following:

1. *Provide students with a combination of written, verbal, and pictorial instructions.* Multiple sensory formats (auditory, visual, kinesthetic) maximize access to science information and learning. In a laboratory, for example, the directions can be depicted in pictures as well as written in text.

2. *Create opportunities for students to work with partners rather than alone, and expect active engagement and participation of all students, including those with disabilities.* Allowing all students to work together, and not forming special groups, sends a strong message about including all students in the learning process and creating a learning environment that values all students.

3. *Extend the time allotted for the inquiry process, including additional time for set-up and clean-up.* Providing additional time will ensure that inquiry lessons are not rushed and that students have adequate time to prepare for, participate in, and contemplate the lesson.

4. *Demonstrate and allow students to engage in aspects of inquiry.* Demonstrating various aspects of inquiry can provide an example about how to engage in inquiry. For example, demonstrating the process by which data is collected and recorded can assist students who have not had the experience previously.

5. *Involve students in the accommodation process to help them be self-advocates in their educational experiences.* Self-advocacy should be explicitly taught and students must practice the process so they will be prepared to assume responsibility for their learning and accommodations later in college. In science classes, because they are required to do both written work and laboratory investigations, students must be able to ask for assistance when they encounter new problems.

6. *Approach the development of accommodations with flexible and creative problem solving.* Science is about flexibility and problem solving. If an accommodation doesn't seem to be working, think of a new approach that may be better or consider a different activity. In other words, don't just talk slower and louder!

7. *Provide diverse role models as guest speakers or as illustrations in curriculum materials so that students can believe that science includes men and women from varied backgrounds and with a range of abilities and disabilities.* In science, role models are important and should be included purposefully. That is, a role model should be presented when he or she can enhance the conversation about science. This conversation can focus on the challenges of doing science with disabilities, as well as the unique strengths scientists have when they do science.

# Conclusion

Science is the perfect course in which to engage and captivate all students. Inquiry instruction, which is at the center of science teaching, can provide a learning experience for all students at any moment. There are objects to touch, see, and smell, and there are investigations to conduct. For students with disabilities these opportunities exist naturally in the inquiry class, and making small revisions to instructional and assessment formats can greatly enhance their learning experiences. Ideally, such modifications can be guided by the ideals presented through a universal design approach. These modifications are not difficult to make and often require a small amount of preparation or the use of common equipment in novel ways (e.g., computers with larger text, meter sticks with raised lines). Once these modifications are made, students can participate more fully in the learning experience, thereby having an impact on their overall performance in science class. Moreover, by providing these learning opportunities to students with disabilities, a clear message is sent that all students can and should participate in science and all students will learn science.

# Scientific Inquiry: The Place of Interpretation and Argumentation 8

Stephen P. Norris, University of Alberta
Linda M. Phillips, University of Alberta
Jonathan F. Osborne, King's College of London

Secondary school students typically believe that scientific inquiry begins with a direct observation of the natural world and that scientific laws and theories become apparent from these observations. Many students even believe that scientific evidence is conclusive *only* if it is directly observable. We know, however, that scientific observation is an interpretation of nature rather than a direct reading and that the movement from observation to laws and theories involves enormous mental and physical effort and resources. Students come by their overly simple view of science from a variety of sources, including science trade books (Ford 2006) and their textbooks.

This chapter suggests how secondary school science education can offer a more accurate picture by emphasizing the role of interpretation and argumentation in scientific inquiry. Interpretation is concerned with questions of meaning and explanation. Argumentation is concerned with justifications of what to conclude and what to do. We provide an extended example demonstrating strategies for making interpretation and argumentation more central to science instruction. We begin, however, with a shorter example to illustrate how the simple view of science is connected to a general misconstrued understanding of learning *as itself simple*—as a process of locating information and memorizing facts. Learning, in this view, is like a conduit, carrying information unobstructed from one person to another. On the contrary, however, all communication is fraught with complexities of comprehension and understanding (see Reddy 1979).

# The Simple View of Learning

Certain common testing practices illustrate well the simple view of learning. Try the following example that mimics standard tests of reading comprehension. Read the passage and answer the multiple-choice questions that follow.

### *Quantum Damping*

*We assumed that the atomic energy levels were infinitely sharp whereas we know from experiment that the observed emission and absorption lines have a finite width. There are many interactions which may broaden an atomic line, but the most fundamental one is the reaction of the radiation field on the atom. That is, when an atom <u>decays</u> spontaneously from an excited state radiatively, it emits a quantum of energy into the radiation field. This radiation may be reabsorbed by the atom. The reaction of the field on the atom gives the atom a linewidth and causes the original level to be shifted. This is the source of the natural linewidth and the Lamb shift.* (Louisell 1973, p. 285)

1. The underlined word <u>decays</u> means: A. splits apart, B. grows smaller, C. gives off energy, D. disappears.

2. According to the passage, observed emission lines are: A. infinitely sharp, B. of different widths, C. of finite width, D. the same width as absorption lines.

3. According to the passage, the most fundamental interaction that may broaden an atomic line is: A. the Lamb shift, B. the action of the atom on the radiation field, C. the emission of a quantum of energy, D. the reaction of the radiation field on the atom.

4. It can be inferred that when an atom decays it may: A. return only to a state more excited than the original one, B. not return to its

original excited state, C. return to its original excited state, D. return to a state less excited than the original one.

5. It can be concluded from the information in this passage that the assumption that atomic energy levels are infinitely sharp is: A. probably false, B. false, C. true, D. still under question.

The correct answers are found at the bottom of this page.

How did you do? Almost everyone who has taken this little test has performed well.

So what is the point? If we constrain learning to the simple view, we must conclude that everyone who performed well on the test learned from reading the passage. They were able to locate information in the text, isolate facts, and answer various inferential questions. Yet, there is a problem with this conclusion. Except for a few, including perhaps some of you, most people who have taken this test do not have the faintest idea what the Quantum Damping passage means.

Performing well on such items—which mimic many items that students face in school—does not imply understanding or learning, because all they test is word recognition and information location. Teaching according to the simple view of learning gives credit for performance that does not require the deep understanding that educators wish students to achieve in science education. As a consequence, students receive an inflated assessment of their ability in science, learn to believe that science does not have to make sense, and acquire a simple view of science.

The purpose of this chapter is to show how student understanding of science concepts can be enhanced through concerted attention to interpretation and argumentation, which are at the core of scientific inquiry.

# Interpretation and Argumentation

Interpretation and argumentation are complementary aspects of scientific inquiry. We are each required to engage in interpretation whenever we wish to go beyond the plain and obvious meaning of something. Interpretation requires judgment and is one of the defining features of inquiry.

Interpretation is *iterative*. It proceeds through a number of stages, each aimed at greater refinement:

---

1-C; 2-C; 3-D; 4-C; 5-B

- Lack of understanding is recognized.

- Alternative interpretations are created.

- Available evidence is used and new evidence is sought as necessary.

- Judgment is suspended until sufficient evidence is available for choosing among the alternatives.

- Interpretations are judged and, when necessary, modified or discarded.

- Alternative interpretations are proposed, sending the process back to the beginning.

Interpretation is also *interactive*. It involves a back-and-forth movement between evidence, the interpreter's background knowledge, existing interpretations, and emerging interpretations. Progress is made by actively imagining new representations of the world—not as it is but as it might be—and then negotiating what is imagined against the evidence and existing background knowledge.

Finally, interpretation is *principled*. The principles are used to weigh and balance conjectured interpretations against the evidence and accepted science. Striving for completeness and consistency are the two main principles. Neither principle is enough by itself, and both must be used in tandem.

Because the meaning of scientific data can never be read directly, any interpretation must be justified with an argument. In the sense we intend, argumentation is the attempt to establish or prove a conclusion on the basis of reasons. A conclusion, in this context, is not simply the end of something; rather, it is a proposition someone is trying to support. *Reasons* is the most general term for the support offered for conclusions. In science, the term *evidence* is often used, especially when the support is provided by data.

However, scientists also provide reasons for what research to pursue, for which data to collect, and for which procedures to use. Moreover, they frequently offer logical arguments for conclusions. Galileo, without appeal to evidence, argued that it is logically inconsistent to claim that heavier objects because of their natures fall at a faster rate than lighter objects. Einstein, also without appeal to evidence, argued that it is logically inconsistent to hold that all observers, regardless of their relative motion, would make the same judgments about the simultaneity of events. In these latter cases, reasons, not data, were brought to bear.

Within the framework of this chapter, an argument is not a dispute. Argumentation, like interpretation, is a defining feature of scientific inquiry (Driver, Newton, and Osborne 2000). Both can be learned with the right experience.

# The Experience Needed

From time to time during their secondary school science education, students need to experience extended inquiries. The aim of these experiences is to show the difficulty and complexity of reaching scientific conclusions. The activities we contemplate emphasize a depth of understanding over a breadth of understanding. Students are asked to linger on a topic, to resist closing off investigation too quickly, and to learn to be more skeptical and less credulous. Generally, they are to attend closely to the reasoning behind scientific understandings and to the interpretation and argumentation involved in securing them.

Extended inquiries can take several forms. In one sort of inquiry, students explore a scientific question starting from its inception, through the research design, data collection, and analysis, to the write-up and presentation of the results. These sorts of inquiries can be valuable, especially when the questions explored come from the students. The approach we describe differs in that it focuses on historical science and questions already settled. The inquiry relies on the teacher making salient for the students the question "How did we come to be so sure?" Students need to feel perplexed, as described in Chapter 4.

The lessons from such activities can be particularly valuable if the conclusion in question is one that students take for granted. These lessons include the following:

- Plants grow by capturing light energy and converting it to chemical energy in a process called "photosynthesis."

- Much of what is now dry land was once under the oceans.

- The heart is a pump that circulates blood throughout the body.

- Water is a compound, each molecule of which is composed of two hydrogen atoms and one oxygen atom.

For each of these conclusions, ready sources of data are available, either through students' own experience, observations, or experiments possible in the high school classroom. However, none of the conclusions is self-evident and arguments must be constructed to justify all of them.

In summary, conditions conducive to showing the place of interpretation and argumentation in scientific inquiry are found in extended activities that

- Emphasize depth over breadth.

- Promote skepticism and challenge credulity.

- Examine everyday and cherished beliefs.

- Have data readily available.

- Can use data from students' observations and experiments.

# An Example of Extended Inquiry

The following is an example of such an activity that builds on the question "Why do we experience day and night on Earth?" A teacher who introduces this as a question in the secondary classroom must first convince students that the question is meant as genuine. Likely, students will produce a quick and certain response that they learned in elementary school: "Day and night are caused by the spinning Earth." You can initiate argumentation by asking something like "How do you know?" or "What makes you so certain of your knowledge?"

Students may provide responses that are legitimate appeals to authority: "My science textbook in eighth grade said so" or "Our teacher two years ago told us this was the reason." However, the point of scientific inquiry is to get students to wonder about the basis for what they know. You could keep the argument alive by asking the students why they believe the textbook or how their former teacher could know the answer, but we recommend another route.

Begin by asking students whether the answer is as self-evident as it seems. After all, during the course of a day, which appears to move—the Sun or the Earth? At this point you have a number of possible routes to follow. The class could be divided into two or more groups, each charged with mustering the most solid case they can for the conclusion. Alternatively, you could facilitate a whole-class discussion. In either arrangement, a good place to start is with *possible* answers to the question. Begin by asking students to imagine that they do not know what causes day and night—indeed that nobody knows the answer. Ask them to think what might be its cause and what evidence and reasoning they can assemble to support their answer. To do that they have to start with conjectures.

# Conjectures

Conjectures are interpretations held tentatively. The mode of thinking involved in conjecturing is central to science: "*If* such-and-such were the case, *would* that explain the phenomenon?" This form of suppositional thinking is hardly ever easy. To the question of what causes night and day, secondary students should be able to imagine the two historical rivals: (1) the Earth spins, making a complete revolution each 24 hours, thus over the course of a day exposing varying parts of its surface to the Sun; and (2) the Sun orbits the Earth once per day, thus shining its light on different parts of the Earth's surface as it does so.

However, the phenomenon of day and night itself is not so cut and dried. Not all days are of equal length; in most places, days are longer in summer, shorter in winter, and in-between lengths in the fall and spring. Further complicating the phenomenon is that the longest days in the Northern Hemisphere correspond to the shortest ones in the Southern Hemisphere and vice versa.

Now the interpretive questions become:

- *If* the Earth were spinning, what would cause days of different length?

- *If* the Sun were orbiting the Earth, what would cause days of different length?

- What in each model would lead to differences between the two hemispheres?

These questions are more difficult to answer, because models that will produce the effects are not easy to imagine. It is important in this phase to help students reflect on what they are doing. They are making tentative interpretations. They are involved in creating ideas and judging whether they *could* explain the phenomenon of day and night. They are holding in abeyance a decision on the truth of those ideas while they pursue available evidence and judge its relevance.

# Relevance

Before the investigation can go much further, the issue of what is relevant must be addressed. A lot is known, but only some of it is pertinent to the question of why there is day and night. You have considerable discretion about when to bring new facts into play. However, it is important to have a number of potentially relevant facts at hand in order to introduce them in a timely fashion as provocations and to sustain the argument. Here are some such facts as an illustration:

- The stars appear to move in a counterclockwise circular direction around Polaris as the approximate center.

- There is seasonal change in the Sun's altitude at noon and in its daily duration in the sky.

- There are monthly phases of the Moon.

- Seasonal transition times vary: spring to summer, 92 days; summer to fall, 94 days; fall to winter, 90 days; winter to spring, 89 days.

Relevance is sometimes difficult to judge, but it is a crucial judgment scientists need to make; otherwise, they will be inundated with more information than they can possibly handle. Students need to learn that judgments of relevance are part of the process of scientific inquiry, and students require practice making them.

Consider the fact that the stars appear to rotate around one fixed star, and imagine students' judging its relevance to the question. Your role is to frame the issue: "Is the fact relevant to the question of what causes night and day? If it is, why? If it is not, why not?" Students are asked not only to make a judgment, but to defend it with reasons.

The demand to provide reasons is what motivates arguments. Students may say that this fact is relevant, because if the Earth were spinning, then the stars would appear to turn. So the fact is evidence that the Earth is spinning. Your role now is to push for deeper thought: "If the Earth were spinning, wouldn't you land on a different spot when you jumped straight up? What would happen if you jumped straight up in an airplane?" The aim in asking these questions is to bring the students to understand that some evidence (where you land when you jump) is irrelevant to deciding whether the Earth is spinning, because it stands neither for nor against the conjecture.

# Evidence

A point that should be made clear to students is that evidence is created through arguments such as those just considered. Evidence is not simply found. It is a fact that the stars appear to move in circular paths. For that fact to become evidence, it must be linked through an argument to an interpretation. The link is that a spinning Earth would create the appearance of stars moving in circular paths around the axis of spin.

That is, if the Earth *were* spinning that would explain the circular motions of the stars as well as the occurrence of day and night. In contrast, the link from the fact of circular star movement to the idea that the Sun orbits the Earth is less direct. An additional and separate conjecture is needed to establish that connection—something like the stars also are spinning with respect to the Earth. According to this conjecture, the motion of the stars would not be apparent, but real.

# Counterevidence

The word *evidence* often is understood only in its positive connotation. Indeed, there is research undertaken by social psychologists showing that there is a confirmation bias in people's reasoning. People tend to see positive evidence but overlook negative evidence, especially when the conjecture under test is a favorite idea (Nisbett and Ross 1980). However, just as there can be evidence *for* a conjecture, there can be evidence *against* it. It is important for students to learn that the surest guard against credulity is the disposition to seek counterevidence—in short, to be skeptical.

What counterevidence could students find against the conjecture that the Earth spins? There are several challenges that can be mounted. If the Earth were spinning, then either it would spin under the air, making all clouds, birds, and other things in the sky appear to be carried the opposite way, or the air would spin, with the Earth making it difficult or impossible for birds and planes to fly against the wind created. That wind speed would be very high all the time, because at the equator the speed of rotation would have to be on the order of 1,600 kph. A spinning Earth would either burst from such motion, literally flying apart, or objects not fixed to the Earth would fly off. Furthermore, if the Earth were spinning, surely you would not land on the same spot when you jumped straight upward. But we know that we do land in the same spot. Students can create even more arguments against the conjecture of the spinning Earth.

Each of these challenges is based upon an interpretation of what would happen were the Earth spinning. Students should be encouraged to provide arguments both for and against these interpretations. That is, the interplay between interpretation and argumentation continues beyond the presentation of evidence and counterevidence, to further arguments—themselves based on evidence—that attempt to counter the counterevidence. In principle, there is no end to how long this back and forth reasoning can proceed. In practice, it ends when scientists conclude that the evidence and argument are sufficient to support one interpretation over the others. Closure, after all, is a goal of science. Scientists move to the next problem once the current one has a coherent solution with sufficient evidence for it.

## Coherence and Sufficient Evidence

Challenge students as follows: "Even if we accept the relevance of the counterclockwise circular motion of the stars and accept that it is evidence for the claim that the Earth spins, is it sufficient evidence? If so, why? If not, why not?" Help students see that the occurrence of day and night cannot be considered in isolation from other phenomena. If day and night are explained by a spinning Earth, we are still left to explain the seasons, the variation in the altitude of the Sun, the opposition of the seasons in the Northern and Southern Hemispheres, the motion and brightness of the planets, and the phases of the Moon. However we explain these additional phenomena, the explanations must be consistent with the idea that it is the Earth that spins, or something must be abandoned.

Students need to learn that interpretations of a single phenomenon rarely can be judged in isolation from the interpretations of other related phenomena. The accepted explanation of the Sun's changing altitude is that the Earth's axis of rotation is tilted 23.5° with respect to the plane of its orbit around the Sun. Some students might cite this explanation, but they should be challenged to show how it works. The comparative merits of a spinning and orbiting Earth on a tilted axis and an orbiting and oscillating Sun can be raised.

## Conclusion

We started by identifying a simple view of science that many students hold even after years of science instruction—that the evidence for scientific beliefs must be directly observable. This misunderstanding of the nature of science is sufficiently problematic that it must be countered. Scientific ideas are imaginative and creative models of objects and processes that often are too small to be seen or too large to be comprehended in a single observation. In short, they are models that must be defended with arguments.

We have proposed a focus on the interpretation and argumentation required to come even to people's most cherished scientific beliefs. For example, nobody, even with all of our space travel, has directly observed that day and night are caused by the spinning Earth (at least nobody from this planet!).

The aim of our extended example was to illustrate how to think about our certainty regarding well-established scientific facts with the purpose of teaching important ideas about science:

- Observation provides only highly inferential access to knowledge.

- All scientific knowledge, even the seemingly simple ideas, is hard won.

Producing this knowledge requires going beyond what our senses tell us and imagining how the world might be. The example showed also that we cannot judge interpretations of one phenomenon without considering many others. Science is an interconnected web of ideas. Tweaking, adding, or removing a strand in one place has ramifications throughout the structure. The rebalancing is a difficult job requiring strategies of interpretation and argumentation:

- Conjectures must be made.

- The relevance of available facts and information must be judged.

- Evidence and counterevidence must be brought to bear upon each conjecture.

- The coherence and sufficiency of the evidence must be assessed.

A major aim of the science curriculum is for students to acquire an understanding of the scientific view of the world and to use scientific reasoning when appropriate. Ironically, this aim is undermined when students commit to memory a great deal of scientific knowledge but grasp little of the grounding for that knowledge, even of the broad shape that grounding might take. We know it is impossible for anyone to know the basis of all the knowledge upon which he or she must be prepared to act. We must accept much of what we know on the basis of credible authority and without ourselves inquiring into the evidence. Wholesale skepticism is debilitating.

Nevertheless, it is important to imbue students with a reasonable level of skepticism; otherwise, they may fall into another equally undesirable frame of mind—credulity. The science classroom is an appropriate site for learning that we can believe too easily and that what appears self-evident often is not. Ask yourself, how you would convince a serious skeptic that matter is made of atoms; that the Earth is not motionless; that nearly all the matter in a tree did not come from the ground; and more?

Science education offers an important context for the critical examination of belief—a frame of mind that is as important outside of science as it is within science. Paying close and detailed attention at least occasionally to the interpretation and argumentation that underwrite even the most taken-for-granted scientific facts is one means for promoting healthy levels of skepticism and for avoiding credulity—in short, for teaching scientific inquiry.

# In Praise of Questions: Elevating the Role of Questions for Inquiry in Secondary School Science

# 9

Catherine Milne, New York University

In science classrooms, teachers and students ask questions for many reasons. Science teachers commonly ask questions to review content with students or to manage classroom interactions. Students' questions are often attempts to make sense of science content or are organizational in nature, often related to issues such as the date for the quiz or the specific content on the test. Rarely in secondary science classrooms are questions asked about the natural world, but such questions are the basis of *doing* science.

*Question posing*, which consists of question generation and evaluation, is essential to the conduct of scientific inquiry. Usually scientific investigations begin with a question generated from experiences with phenomena. Helping secondary students identify and construct questions that promote scientific inquiry is important and explicitly called for in the National Science Education Standards (NRC 1996). Moreover, identifying and constructing questions help students recognize the central role of questions in science and help students become more effective inquirers. So the initial impetus for question posing is to provide learning environments where students can interact with phenomena.

If scientific inquiry is to be part of the focus in secondary school science, teachers must develop learning situations in which question posing is essential and they must help students learn how to pose scientifically oriented questions. In focusing on questions, teachers and students both play an important role in the classroom. Teachers provide rich inquiry-based opportunities for students, while students engage in exploring the phenomena they encounter in class.

# Creating a Learning Environment for Question Posing

## Use a Question Focus Rather Than an Answer Focus

Much secondary school science focuses on the products of scientific inquiry. This focus obscures the importance of questions in inquiry, the importance of phenomena to build science knowledge, and the role that theory plays in the questions that can be asked. In this context, science knowledge or phenomena are presented at the beginning of a unit or lesson, which gives students few opportunities to ask questions. Students need opportunities to pose questions that help them develop an understanding of phenomena in nature that includes facts, models, laws, and theories.

In adopting a question focus, teachers can use introductory experiences to elicit questions from students. For instance, before discussing or lecturing about chemical reactions, a teacher could have students complete the activity described in Figure 9.1. This experience encourages students to propose a range of questions that

FIGURE 9.1. QUESTION-GENERATING ACTIVITY

**Overarching Question: What drives chemical reactions?**

Measure out 7 grams of citric acid and 10 grams of sodium bicarbonate and then mix these compounds in a plastic bag that can be closed. When the compounds are mixed, put a thermometer into the mixture and record the temperature. Measure out 10 ml of water into a small container and make sure the outside of the container is dry. Carefully place the container with water in the plastic bag without spilling water. Close the bag around the thermometer, and then tip over the container of water in the bag and observe any changes that take place. Record any questions that come to you during your observations. After 10 minutes, clean up as directed by the teacher.

orient them to the topic of chemical reactions. Other types of initial experiences include a demonstration, a reading of a scientific study, or close observations of the community outside of school or of phenomena inside the classroom.

# Elicit Questions From Experiences

In science, questions to be investigated come from scientists' ongoing involvement with phenomena and theories about which they have both interest and experience. Similarly, as students become involved with phenomena, they ask questions related to their experience. The example in Figure 9.1 can illustrate this point. When first confronted with the phenomenon, students can write questions that come to them as they observe the reaction, such as, "Why was the mixture boiling?" and "How did the ice get in the container?" These questions originate from the prior experiences of the students, and their tentative answers may not align with the scientifically accepted explanation. The orientation toward asking questions allows students to reveal their level of understanding about the topic and encourages them to generate an interest in the topic. However, proposing questions is only the beginning. Students need questions they can investigate, which leads us to the next point...

# Develop Questions That Can Be Investigated

Sometimes initial questions cannot be answered directly because they are too broad to investigate (e.g., "How does the human brain work?"). Broad questions, however, can provide the starting point for questions more amenable to investigation. In this example, understanding the mechanisms associated with the brain can result in a focus on brain activity, learning, speaking, or memory. In addressing these questions, scientists often work with model organisms (such as mice and roundworms) to answer specific questions.

Additionally, some questions can be answered with a quick Web search or by examining reference material. Such narrow questions often have a predetermined answer that may not be appropriate for students to investigate. Finally, some questions are not related to science. Questions such as, "Which paper towel is the best?" or "What color is best to wear to the prom?" do not address phenomena in nature (see Chapter 1 for a discussion on this point). Ultimately, questions in science need to be focused, involve the collection of data, and be related to nature.

# Questions to Ask in the Science Classroom

Questions help students negotiate the tricky terrain between experiencing the phenomenon and the final explanation. Broadly, questions in science are associated with looking for patterns in nature and developing and using theories and models that explain phenomena in nature. In this section, the focus is on questions related to experiences of phenomena. Using different types of questions contributes to a student's understanding of a concept. *Definition questions* help students identify events that are well accepted in the science community. *Experimental questions* allow students to explore how variables are linked to one another. *Observational questions* give students a chance to explore patterns that exist in nature. Collectively, these types of questions are different avenues for exploring phenomena, leading to different conclusions (see Table 9.1).

## Definition Questions

Definition questions correspond to an investigational process, resulting in answers that are accepted in the scientific community and that are usually shared prior to an investigation. The questions provided in Table 9.1 correspond to chemistry and result in answers that are reported in textbooks or other curricular materials. It might appear that definition questions should not be pursued by students because they can simply confirm known ideas. These questions should be investigated, though, because they can allow students to construct their own knowledge about the topic. For the science teacher, the challenge of getting students to generate these questions is (a) to refrain from providing the answer first and (b) to provide an event that can serve as a starting point for additional investigations.

These types of questions can lead to different questions that can be pursued in the science classroom. For example, when students pursue the question "Is water necessary for the reaction to occur?" they can expand on their findings to identify additional questions exploring concentration, composition, or reaction rates. These types of questions can be experimental or observational in nature. Developing concept maps or word webs related to their conclusions will help students create different questions. More importantly, when students generate their own questions, they are often more interested in answering them, and their practice is more consistent with the practice of science.

TABLE 9.1. TYPES OF QUESTIONS AND METHODS OF INQUIRY

| Question Type | Sample Questions | Method of Inquiry | Forms of Appropriate Answers |
|---|---|---|---|
| Definition | What is the gaseous product?<br><br>What type of reaction is this? | Observing a phenomenon and relating it to an idea in science | Definitions |
| Experimental | How does changing the concentration of one chemical impact the reaction rate?<br><br>What temperature ensures that the reaction will be completed in the least amount of time? | Exploring the empirical relationship between the dependent and independent variable | Cause and effect relationships |
| Observational | How is the reaction similar to the reaction of an instantaneous ice pack?<br><br>What would have happened if we used a solvent other than water? | Using direct and instrumental observation of phenomena to identify possible relationships | Correlations and classifications |

# Experimental Questions

Experimental questions correspond to strategic observations of events and often include specific variables. These variables are defined as the independent variable, which is manipulated by the experimenter, and the dependent variable, which responds to the independent variable. These types of experiments are a result of the refinement of science over time and reflect the manipulation of nature to obtain better findings (Carnap 1995). It should also be noted that the findings from these types of questions rarely overturn long-standing or accepted scientific theories, but they contribute to the ongoing development of the model or theory.

Experimental questions help students develop supported explanations, which emerge from designed experiments. Glickstein (2002) provided a good example of an experimental question that can have competing explanations. When Glickstein was in junior high school, his science teacher placed a burning candle under a jar. The candle was standing in a tray of water, and as the candle went out, water rushed in and seemed to occupy the space in the jar. His teacher told the class that the space occupied by the water was 20% of the total space under the jar, thereby confirming that the candle went out because as it burned it used all the oxygen and the water rushed in to take up the space formerly occupied by the oxygen. As a consequence of this demonstration, Glickstein investigated other questions that challenged this conclusion and ultimately determined that the teacher's explanation was incorrect. For instance, adding more candles (independent variable) resulted in more water (dependent variable) filling the jar, not just 20% of the space. In the end, the explanation offered by Glickstein aligned with theories about heat, pressure, and the movement of particles.

# Observational Questions

Questions that don't manipulate nature and use observations as sources of information are observational questions. These questions often come about when a student notices an anomaly or irregularity in the natural world. Observations generate ideas about the phenomenon and lead to a question that requires additional observations. Once developed, observational questions require as many observations as possible. When enough data are collected to allow for a conclusion that describes the event, the conclusion will often describe a pattern or a connection. More importantly, the patterns or relationships that emerge come from an "onlooker" as opposed to a person manipulating the natural world (Carnap 1995). These types of investigations are limited, as conducting all the observations necessary to make a robust conclusion is impossible.

Observational questions are important in describing regularities in nature and can lead to additional investigations. Often, observational questions can be the precursor to experimental questions. Take, for instance, the observations often made by students trying to understand the different phases of matter. Such an investigation can begin with ice and then the ice changing to water and then water vapor. In watching these changes, students may conclude that water can occur in different phases and elect to watch other materials change phase. After watching different substances change phase, students may conclude that matter can exist in a solid, liquid, or gas state. But this is just the beginning. With further exploration, students may raise questions about optimal points in which matter changes phase, which may result in an experiment that pursues descriptions of various phase changes.

## Questions in the Larger Context

In science, questions are essential. For instance, those engaged in science ask questions prior to engaging in an exploration. As data are collected, questions are asked about the data, the phenomena, and the process by which data are collected. When data are analyzed, there are questions about the process used to examine the data, the method used to represent the data, the findings that are important to the study, and the means used to present information to the recipients. There are also questions about how the study fits with the proposed theory, as investigations support the development of theories. Because science is about questions, science in the secondary classroom should also focus on questions.

When the teacher begins a process of scientific inquiry, his or her first question is not the question that becomes the focus of the inquiry, but an invitation to inquiry. If students are to develop a richer understanding of inquiry, then the teacher needs to assist them in developing questions that can be addressed using scientific inquiry. The strategies for generating questions outlined in this chapter can be used in all science courses taught in secondary school. Once students have generated different questions, teachers can revisit Table 9.1 and ask, "What type of question do we have and what does that mean about the methods we might use to answer this question?" The answer to this question will set students on the path to different inquiries.

There are challenges associated with creating learning environments in which secondary students are encouraged to ask questions about phenomena. Question posing is a skill that requires continual use and refinement, and it should remain a focus for all levels of education. If scientific inquiry is to be part of the focus in secondary school, students must be taught about the types of questions that serve to guide scientific inquiry, how these questions can be developed, and how they are interrelated to one another. In short, teachers need to develop learning situations that allow students to ask different types of questions, just as they do in science.

# Assessing Science as Inquiry in the Classroom

**Pamela Van Scotter, BSCS (Biological Sciences Curriculum Study)**
**K. David Pinkerton, BSCS**

Inquiry is essential to scientific endeavors. Consequently, it is essential that students understand and use it. Several previous chapters of this book have described how questions, explanations, argumentation, and interpretation are aspects of inquiry that should be part of school science instruction. Other chapters have provided glimpses of what inquiry might look like in specific contexts, such as in a chemistry class or an Earth science class. Now that some clear models for inquiry-based instruction have been established, this chapter will describe some ideas about assessing for understandings and abilities related to inquiry.

Teachers need to have strong ideas about what will serve as evidence of students' understanding of inquiry before they begin teaching (Wiggins and Mc-Tighe 2005). Once teachers know what will serve as evidence for understanding, then sequencing effective learning experiences can be more targeted and more clearly focused.

# Assessing Inquiry and Links to How Students Learn

When assessing students' understandings of and abilities in regard to inquiry, teachers should ensure that the assessments align with instruction and with the current findings about how students learn. Using Table 10.1, consider some characteristics of inquiry assessments that are consistent with the research of Bransford, Brown, and Cocking (2000).

TABLE 10.1. ASSESSING FOR INQUIRY CONSISTENT WITH KEY FINDINGS ABOUT LEARNING

| Key Findings From *How People Learn** | Implications for Assessing Science as Inquiry |
|---|---|
| 1. Learners come to the classroom with conceptions about the world around them. | • Assessments should provide opportunities for students to demonstrate what they know and what they don't know about scientifically testable questions, designing investigations, using evidence to develop explanations, and communicating findings to others. |
| 2. Learners need a deep foundation of conceptual knowledge upon which to build improved understandings. | • Assessments need to be conceptually coherent and connected to the students' current foundation of understandings of and abilities in regard to science as inquiry.<br><br>• Assessments need to be ongoing so as to continually add layers to the foundation of knowledge and abilities related to inquiry.<br><br>• Assessments need to be balanced to provide a complete picture of what students know. |
| 3. Learners need opportunities to monitor their own learning. | • Assessments need to provide students with opportunities to assess themselves in ways that help them monitor how strong their understanding is and at what point it begins to break down.<br><br>• Assessments need to be relevant and compelling so that students will see the value in monitoring their understanding. |

*The findings in column one are adapted from Bransford, J. D., A. L. Brown, and R. R. Cocking, eds. 2000. *How people learn: Brain, mind, experience, and school.* Washington, DC: National Academy Press, pp. 14–18.

# Balanced Assessments of Inquiry

Teachers should ensure that assessments of inquiry are balanced and authentic. By *balanced,* we mean that teachers should assess the many ways and the many points at which students represent what they know or are in the process of learning about science as inquiry. By *authentic,* we mean that the assessments should reflect the nature of science and the practice of the scientific endeavor.

## Balanced Assessments Include a Range of Assessment Types

As a first step, consider the types of assessments that, taken together, make up a balanced approach. Using the principles of backward design (Wiggins and McTighe 2005), these assessment types follow from the desired outcomes of inquiry (NRC 1996), as shown in Table 10.2.

TABLE 10.2. OUTCOMES OF INQUIRY ALIGNED WITH A RANGE OF ASSESSMENT TYPES

| Targeted Outcome of Inquiry | Assessment Type | How Outcome Aligns With Assessment Type |
|---|---|---|
| Understanding about inquiry | Endpoint (summative, point-in-time, static, delayed feedback) | Inquiry is a body of knowledge that can be tested objectively after instruction. |
| Ability to perform inquiry | Dynamic (formative, ongoing feedback, "in the moment") | Inquiry is a process that can be monitored and evaluated as students perform it. |
| Conceptual under-standing | Conceptual frame-work (cognitive associations, mental structures, conceptual connections) | Inquiry produces changes in students' conceptual frameworks, moving them toward more expert-like thinking. |

*Endpoint assessments* evaluate what students know at a single point in time, usually after instruction. For example, tests and quizzes give teachers information on how students respond to classroom activities. Typically, endpoint assessments require students to interact with nonchanging (static) prompts, such as multiple-choice or free-response questions. Feedback from teacher to student is delayed. Endpoint assessments make it difficult for teachers to know exactly what students are thinking, especially when written responses are sparse or difficult to interpret. These assessments do provide important objective documentation of a student's abilities at a moment in time, however.

*Dynamic assessments* determine how students respond to changing (dynamic) prompts. For example, teachers use questions in conversations with students to pinpoint what they can answer on their own and what they need help to answer. The fluid nature of teacher-student, real-time feedback provides information for ongoing learning (see Vygotsky 1962/1986). The same type of back-and-forth interactions occur among students during investigations (Hake 1992). This is especially true when teachers orchestrate conversational prompts to probe students' prior conceptions, to link evidence and interpretation, or to construct meaning through argumentation and inference. Student notebooks also provide a record of these "in the moment" interactions. Teachers can use notebooks to assess the ongoing aspects of student learning (as described in Biological Sciences Curriculum Study [BSCS] 1994).

*Conceptual framework assessments* give teachers insight into the way students store, retrieve, and associate knowledge. For example, the concept maps and graphic organizers of experts in a field are consistently different from novices (see Novak 1990). The association and hierarchy of concepts form the basis of mental structures used to do well in school. Cognitive framework assessments inform teachers about the effect their teaching has on those structures.

## Designing Balanced Assessments

One way to ensure a balanced approach to assessment is to design a scoring scheme or rubric that reflects the desired balance among endpoint, dynamic, and conceptual framework assessments. This way, teachers have data so they can effectively triangulate what students know and can do. As a result, teachers can improve their ability to individualize instruction.

For example, imagine a unit on designing, conducting, and communicating results of a scientific investigation. How do you construct a balanced rubric for this unit on inquiry? Naturally, assessing inquiry works best and most efficiently within a context, namely, specific science content. For this example on assessing inquiry, consider the following focus question posed to students: "What affects the period of a pendulum and how?" Note that in a "full" inquiry students would formulate their own questions, but in many actual school circumstances, time constraints do not allow full inquiry in every activity. Nonetheless, each aspect of inquiry can be assessed, documented, and used to guide instruction.

Before students begin their investigation, the teacher communicates all assessment criteria in the form of a scoring rubric. The rubric tells students ahead of time what is important and what a high-quality performance looks like. Rubrics accomplish this, in part, by reflecting the intended balance of assessment types. The inherent balance structured into the rubric sends a clear message to students about what is essential to learn. In other words, if you say balance is important, then it should be assessed in student performance.

How do you build a balanced rubric? A rubric *design matrix* can help ensure a balanced assessment. Think of a design matrix as systematic brainstorming. That is, creatively generate ideas for assessments by thinking of examples from specific categories of assessment. In the design matrix, list the concrete tasks to be assessed in the task column. Generally, only one task for each category of assessment is necessary.

Next, form questions that a specific assessment type would tend to answer. Note that students will not have to answer all questions from each category of assessment. The intent at this stage is to generate as many questions per category as possible, as in a brainstorming activity. Eventually, convert some of these questions into concrete, performance-level indicators associated with specific tasks. These performance criteria show up in the final rubric.

Since the assessment categories represent, in sum, a balanced assessment, then chances are good that the final rubric will also be balanced. When the rubric is balanced and students use the rubric to guide their work, chances are that the work students do will also be balanced. Table 10.3 is a completed rubric design matrix for the pendulum-period activity.

After filling each cell in the design matrix, use the completed matrix to decide the best match between task and assessment type. For example, in Table 10.2, the individual multiple-choice test best aligns with endpoint assessments. Eventually, each task is assessed by one type of assessment. Of course, there is overlap, but you decide what the final division will be. A balanced assessment results from spreading the types of assessment among the tasks on the rubric and giving significant weight to each assessment type in scoring. Finally, write performance-level indicators for each task and decide how to weight each task for scoring purposes.

The rubric in Table 10.4 results from the design matrix just discussed. In this rubric, teachers use the concept map task to assess conceptual framework knowledge, the multiple-choice test as an endpoint assessment, and documentation in students' notebooks (along with teacher observations during

TABLE 10.3. EXAMPLE OF A DESIGN MATRIX THAT HELPS ENSURE A BALANCED
ASSESSMENT FOR A GIVEN TASK

| Task | Endpoint | Dynamic | Conceptual Framework |
|---|---|---|---|
| Generate, complete, and evaluate the results of a systematic procedure to answer the focus question. | • Does the student produce a procedure?<br><br>• Does the student carry out the procedure?<br><br>• Does the student evaluate the results? | • Are there various drafts of the procedure in the student's notebook?<br><br>• Are there notes from discussions during design iterations?<br><br>• Do you see evidence of ongoing adjustments to the design, based on feedback from others? From the phenomenon?<br><br>• Is there evidence of an emerging conclusion based on ongoing evaluation? | • Does the student use the language of inquiry properly?<br><br>• Does the student use the focus question to make decisions about steps in the design?<br><br>• Does the student construct conclusions based on evidence? Are they logical and consistent? |
| Take individual multiple-choice test regarding essential understandings about inquiry. | • What is the raw percent correct? | • How much time was required?<br><br>• Did the student request clarification or elaboration during test?<br><br>• What appears on the scratch paper? | • What type of questions were missed most often (conceptual, algorithmic, or recall)?<br><br>• How does distribution of missed items compare to highest-performing students? |

*Table 10.3 continues on next page.*

*Table 10.3 continued.*

| Task | Endpoint | Dynamic | Conceptual Framework |
|------|----------|---------|----------------------|
| Review and analyze a research article about the essential understandings of scientific investigations. | • Are there notes in the student's notebook?<br><br>• Did the student list key words in the notebook?<br><br>• Can the student write an effective summary paragraph analyzing the research and the findings? | • Do students use literacy strategies during reading?<br><br>• Do students debrief with peers about the article?<br><br>• Are there notes from peer debriefings that indicate thoughtful discussion? | • Can the student generate a concept map using essential terms of the article?<br><br>• Does concept map demonstrate coherent principles and conceptual connections?<br><br>• Is the extent and sense of relatedness among concepts similar to what teacher-experts might produce? |

lab) to focus on dynamic assessment. The end product is a balanced assessment from which teachers produce a balanced learning environment—one most capable of enhancing achievement for a broad diversity of learners.

# Authentic Assessment: Capturing Information About Students' Practice of Science

To more fully assess and monitor students' abilities of inquiry in the classroom, teachers and students can use the same type of rubric presented in Table 10.4 but in this case—Table 10.5 on page 116—designed specifically to focus on these abilities of inquiry (NRC 2000). So, for example, throughout a year or a semester, students can set goals for themselves and monitor their progress toward these goals. Teachers also can use such a rubric to formally assess students' performances on a specific investigation, as well as to

TABLE 10.4. EXAMPLE OF A BALANCED SCORING RUBRIC

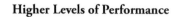

**Higher Levels of Performance**

| Weight | Task | 3 | 2 | 1 |
|---|---|---|---|---|
| 40% | Design, conduct, and evaluate the results of an investigation to answer the focus question. | Exhibits detailed ongoing progress of design process by documenting the development of procedures, the responses to peer feedback, and the generation of conclusions in notebook. | Documents and exhibits an understanding of the final design only, not ideas and drafts of ongoing design development. | Records data from investigation with little reference to ongoing procedural adjustments and developing interpretations of data. |
| 30% | Take individual multiple-choice test regarding essential understandings about inquiry. | Selects between 81% and 100% of the multiple-choice answers correctly. | Selects between 61% and 80% of the multiple-choice answers correctly. | Selects between 0% and 60% of the multiple-choice answers correctly. |
| 30% | Create a concept map, demonstrating a rigorous review and analysis of an article about the essential understandings of inquiry. | Designs, generates, and explains a concept map containing key ideas related to understandings of inquiry, which reflect article's conceptual hierarchy, connectedness, and application. | Constructs concept map with key concept terms, but does not show and explain the hierarchy, connectedness, or application among those terms from the article. | Produces a physical arrangement of terms from the article that has little discernible rationale and does not reflect hierarchy, connectedness, or application of the key understandings of inquiry. |

*Note*: The balanced scoring rubric weights each task sufficiently to communicate the importance of all outcomes to students.

discern patterns of strengths or weaknesses across the class. These assessment practices align with the goals for assessment outlined in Table 10.1. This type of information helps a teacher structure the subsequent learning experiences to target the type of practice and feedback students need most.

# The Influence of Instructional Models

Constructivist instructional models represent an example of a family of instructional models that, among other things, foster balanced and authentic assessment. Such models orchestrate learning for students in a way that supports enduring understandings and provides a framework for constructing knowledge about scientific inquiry (Bybee 1997). Specific examples can help demonstrate the ways in which stages of an instructional model are linked to different types of assessment and how these assessments are also learning opportunities for students.

In the invitation or engagement phase of an instructional model, as well as during the discovery or exploration phase, opportunities for dynamic assessments of abilities and understandings of inquiry are introduced. For example, imagine that Ms. Washington, a middle school science teacher, had assigned her students the task of designing an investigation as part of ongoing class activities. She can now become part of the assessment process through dialogue with students, especially in the form of questions. She can monitor the design process by observing student interactions, reviewing student notebooks, and evaluating the activity results.

As part of monitoring the design process, she would involve herself in informal feedback sessions with students. Then she would use the trajectory of these interactions to assess the dynamic (ongoing) growth in a student's inquiry abilities. Examine the following dynamic assessment version of Ms. Washington's design task and look for evidence of in-the-moment learning.

S:   Ms. Washington, what do we do next? You didn't give us a worksheet with the steps.

T:   Does the focus question give you any ideas?

S:   It just asks what happens to volume if temperature changes. It doesn't say what to do.

T:   How did you know to *change* temperature? The question didn't have that in there.

TABLE 10.5. SAMPLE COMPLETED RUBRIC

**Higher Levels of Performance**

| Weight | Features of Inquiry* | 3 | 2 | 1 |
|---|---|---|---|---|
| 15% | Engages in scientifically oriented questions. | Consistently recognizes and poses appropriate questions that can be answered by science. | Is sometimes able to recognize and pose appropriate questions. | Rarely distinguishes between questions that can and cannot be answered by science. |
| 25% | Gives priority to evidence as he or she explores answers to questions. | Consistently understands and determines what appropriate evidence is and designs investigations to collect it. | Is sometimes able to determine what evidence is needed to answer simple questions and design simple investigations. | Rarely is able to determine what evidence is needed to answer a question or to design an investigation to collect it. |
| 25% | Formulates explanations based on evidence. | Evaluates the evidence critically and consistently uses appropriate evidence to formulate explanations. | Formulates intermediate explanations using mostly appropriate evidence. | Formulates weak explanations, often using unrelated evidence. |
| 25% | Connects his or her new explanations to a rich base of current knowledge. | Seeks out additional information and connects it appropriately to current explanations. | Seeks out other information but is not able to connect it to current explanation. | Rarely connects information from other sources. |
| 10% | Communicates and justifies the explanations he or she constructs. | Develops and communicates a logically consistent explanation. | Develops an intermediate explanation that includes some inconsistencies or uses only partial evidence. | Develops a weak explanation that is logically inconsistent and uses little evidence. |

*Note*: This rubric represents a tool for both students and teachers as they observe the students' inquiry abilities improve during the year.

*The Features of Inquiry in column two are adapted from National Research Council (NRC). 2000. *Inquiry and the national science education standards: A guide for teaching and learning.* Washington, DC: National Academy Press.

S:    How else are we supposed to make the volume do something?

T:    Good thinking, Eddie, you have to change the temperature. Write down how you're going to do that in steps that other students could follow.

S:    Is that all we have to do?

T:    Well, what else have you done when you have designed investigations in class?

S:    Let's see. We've been careful to change the thing we want to study and keep the other things the same.

T:    OK, now you're putting some good ideas together. Try putting those ideas in your design. Then call me over and we'll talk some more.

Ms. Washington didn't accept Eddie's initial knowledge position as an accurate reflection of his true ability. So she thought of questions to probe Eddie's deeper understanding. In Eddie's first response, she noticed how Eddie had inferred the need for a change in temperature from the focus question. Then she prompted specific actions (writing a design and procedure) that caused Eddie to formalize and record his thinking. Finally, she foreshadowed the need for continued feedback as she and Eddie worked toward a finished design.

At the end of an explanation-type activity, a teacher might ask, "Which of the following is a question that can be answered by science?" If a student chooses an incorrect response such as, "Is it right to euthanize unwanted dogs?" the response informs the teacher about the student's specific understandings regarding inquiry. This type of feedback often comes at the end of an activity when students have been developing their understandings and explanations, and so this is an example endpoint assessment.

Application and evaluation-type lessons can be used to assess changes in students' conceptual frameworks. We know that this is a critical first step in learning (see Bransford, Brown, and Cocking 2000). For example, to engage students' prior knowledge about using evidence to develop explanations, the teacher might have the students construct a concept map using their current understanding of the importance of evidence. After progressing through conceptually coherent, carefully sequenced activities, students would be asked to construct another concept map from the same concept words. By comparing the before and after maps to an "expert" map, teachers can validly assess changes in the conceptual framework of their students (Pinkerton 1998). Other forms of assessing aspects of changes in students' conceptual framework include performance on conceptually oriented tests, generating graphic organizers that convey a conceptual hierarchy and connectiveness, and solving open-ended problems, such as those typically found in authentic assessments.

# Student Self-Assessment: When Inquiry Gets Personal

Balanced and authentic approaches to assessing inquiry teach students about multiple sources of feedback, not just feedback from the teacher. One of the most important sources of feedback is when students monitor their own thinking (metacognition) (Bransford, Brown, and Cocking 2000). This monitoring reflects the important goals for assessment outlined in Table 10.1 that link assessment to what we know about learning. Self-assessment involves an ongoing and iterative interaction with the prompt at hand, be it a reading, an investigation, or an open-ended project. Students use the information they obtain from self-monitoring to assess their understanding and adjust their learning paths. The use of a rubric such as the ones in Tables 10.4 and 10.5 are useful tools for students in this process. In many ways, the active meta "dialogue" required by student self-assessment is at the heart of effective inquiry.

Using dynamic and conceptual framework assessments in addition to endpoint assessments teaches students self-assessment skills. For example, consider what it takes to teach students how to learn from mistakes. It requires explicit instruction on how to pinpoint, articulate, and remedy mistakes on content-related activities. In effect, students who learn from mistakes learn to monitor their ongoing thinking and use it to plan actions and solve problems. Used with unit tests, learning from mistakes through self-assessment and peer dialogue shifts endpoint assessments toward dynamic assessments and fosters greater balance and higher achievement (Pinkerton 2005).

When students learn and practice self-assessment skills, they move toward greater intellectual independence. They tend not to require as much external feedback from teachers and can chart their own way through an investigation. In turn, teachers can allot more of their time to those students who still are struggling, thus spending time where it is most needed. In effect, teaching self-assessment skills shrinks the class size by increasing the number of students who can apply the outcomes of inquiry to doing the business of school.

# Conclusion

The message is clear—the ability of students to understand and to do inquiry is essential. Developing inquiry-based lessons and assessing for understandings and abilities of inquiry go hand in hand. In fact, well-designed inquiry-based lessons result from well-designed assessments—ones focused on the important features of inquiry. This backward design approach begins with the end (the assessment), which in turn, provides a specific target for the learning sequence that builds toward the assessment task. That is, the process begins with what is important for students to know (the essential skills and understandings of inquiry) and ends up with an effective learning environment (the day-to-day experiences that shape what students know and understand).

Assessments of inquiry should align with what we know about learning and should be balanced and authentic. That is, they should include all the important features of inquiry, not just those easy to assess. This approach helps ensure that all students acquire the knowledge of and skills regarding scientific inquiry considered important. In turn, this foundation of knowledge should help students participate more effectively in an increasingly complex world.

# Inquiry and Scientific Explanations: Helping Students Use Evidence and Reasoning

**11**

Katherine L. McNeill, Boston College
Joseph Krajcik, University of Michigan

Science is fundamentally about explaining phenomena by determining how or why they occur and the conditions and consequences of the observed phenomena. For example, ecologists may try to explain why species diversity is decreasing in an ecosystem, or astronomers may try to explain the phases of the Moon based on the relative positions of the Sun, Earth, and Moon. When scientists explain phenomena and construct new claims, they provide evidence and reasons to justify them or to convince other scientists of the validity of the claims.

To be scientifically literate citizens, students need to engage in similar inquiry. They need to understand and evaluate explanations that appear in newspapers, in magazines, and on the news to determine their credibility and validity. For example, a newspaper article may claim that stem cell research is important for human health and for treating diseases. Students need to be able to critically read that article by evaluating the evidence and reasoning presented in it. That capability allows students to make informed decisions.

Students should also support their own written claims with appropriate justification. Science education should help prepare students for this complex inquiry practice where students seek and provide evidence and reasons for ideas or claims (Driver, Newton, and Osborne 2000).

In this chapter, we describe the importance of scientific explanation in inquiry, common difficulties students have in justifying their claims, and a suggested instructional approach for supporting students in writing scientific explanations.

We then discuss five instructional strategies teachers can use to support students in scientific explanation, including transcripts from classroom discussions (collected during our research) to illustrate what these strategies look like in actual classrooms.

# Why Scientific Explanation?

National science education standards (AAAS 1993; NRC 1996) and science education researchers (Sandoval and Reiser 2003; Windschitl, see Chapter 1) emphasize the importance of having students construct evidence-based scientific explanations as essential to scientific inquiry. For example, one standard described in *Benchmarks for Scientific Literacy* (AAAS 1993) states, "Scientific investigations usually involve the collection of relevant evidence, the use of logical reasoning, and the application of imagination in devising hypotheses and explanations to make sense of the collected evidence" (p. 12).

Repeatedly, the National Science Education Standards (NSES) (NRC 1996) stress the importance of developing explanations using evidence. In a section on understandings about scientific inquiry, the NSES state, "Scientists evaluate the explanations proposed by other scientists by examining evidence, comparing evidence, identifying faulty reasoning, pointing out statements that go beyond the evidence, and suggesting alternative explanations for the same observations" (p. 148). These standards highlight the key role of explanation in scientific inquiry.

Engaging students in explanation and argumentation can result in numerous benefits for students. For example, creating and supporting their claims can help students develop a stronger understanding of the content knowledge (Zohar and Nemet 2002). When students construct explanations, they actively use the scientific principles to explain different phenomena, developing a deeper understanding of the content. Constructing explanations may also help change students' views of science (Bell and Linn 2000). Often students view science as a static set of facts that they need to memorize. They do not understand that scientists socially construct scientific ideas and that this science knowledge can change over time. By engaging in this inquiry practice, students can also improve their ability to justify their own written claims (McNeill et al. 2006).

Although scientific explanation is an essential learning goal, students often have difficulty articulating and defending their claims (Sadler 2004). For example, they struggle to provide appropriate evidence for their claims and to provide reasoning that describes why their evidence supports their claims (McNeill and Krajcik In press-a). Instead, students tend to write claims without providing any justification for them. This is not surprising, since engaging students in justifying their claims is not often called for in science classrooms (Kuhn 1993), and curriculum materials do not provide teachers with concrete support on how to help students with this complex inquiry practice.

# What Is Scientific Explanation?

In our work with teachers, we have developed an instructional approach to support students in writing scientific explanation (McNeill et al. 2006; Moje et al. 2004). This instructional approach builds on previous science educators' research on students' constructions of scientific explanations (Sandoval and Reiser 2003) and arguments (Bell and Linn 2000; Jiménez-Aleixandre, Rodríguez, and Duschl 2000; Norris, Phillips, and Osborne, this volume, Chapter 8), as well as Toulmin's (1958) model of argumentation. Although we built from research on both explanation and argumentation, we chose the phrase *scientific explanation* to align with the NSES, which the teachers we work with need to address.

The explanation framework includes three components: a claim, evidence, and reasoning. The *claim* makes an assertion or conclusion that addresses the original question or problem about a phenomenon. The *evidence* supports the student's claim using scientific data. This data can come from an investigation that students complete or from another source, such as observations, reading material, or archived data, and needs to be both appropriate and sufficient to support the claim. By *appropriate,* we mean data that are relevant to the problem and help determine and support the claim. *Sufficient* refers to providing enough data to convince another individual of the claim. Often providing sufficient evidence requires using multiple pieces of data. The *reasoning* links the claim and evidence and shows why the data count as evidence to support the claim. Often in order to make this link, students must apply appropriate scientific principles.

In this chapter, we draw examples from our work (see McNeill et al. 2004) to illustrate students' written explanations and instructional strategies that teachers use to support students. This unit, which we call the "Stuff" unit, engages students in the study of substances and properties, the nature of chemical reactions, and the conservation of matter. In the Stuff unit, we contextualize the concepts and scientific inquiry in real-world experience, such as making soap from fat. Although our examples come from our observations of teachers using the Stuff unit, other teachers have used the scientific explanation framework to successfully support students in other content areas and at various grade levels.

During the Stuff unit, students complete many tasks in which they are asked to construct scientific explanations. One of the items asks students to explain a particular phenomenon. They examine a data table and determine whether any of the liquids are the same substance (see Appendix A, p. 134). Figure 11.1 is the response from one student for this question.

FIGURE 11.1. EXAMPLE OF A 7TH-GRADE STUDENT'S SCIENTIFIC EXPLANATION

**Write a scientific explanation** that states whether any of the liquids are the same substance.

> Liquid 1 and 4 are indeed the same substances Looking at this data, the properties include Density, Color, and Melting Point. Mass is not a property. Density, color and M.P. are all the same for liquid 1 and 4. Since all of these propeties are the same, 1 and 4 are the same substance.

This example illustrates a strong scientific explanation from a 7th-grade student. This student provided an accurate claim that liquids 1 and 4 are the same substance. She included multiple pieces of appropriate evidence (density, color, and melting point) to support her claim. She also provided her reasoning for why her data counted as evidence to support her claim. She wrote, "Looking at this data, the properties include density, color, and melting point. Mass is not a property." This tells why she used some data as evidence (density, color, and melting point) and did not use other data (mass). Then she articulated the general science principle (since properties are the same, they are the same substance) that allowed her to select her evidence and support her claim. Although this example provides a relatively simple scientific explanation, students can use the same framework to guide their responses in more complex writing tasks.

To help this student write a scientific explanation in which she appropriately justified her claim, she was given numerous supports and scaffolds in the curriculum during the Stuff unit and from her teacher. The remainder of this chapter focuses on different strategies teachers have used to support their students.

# How Can Teachers Support Students in Writing Scientific Explanations?

Teachers are essential for supporting students in scientific inquiry practices. From recent research on learning and instruction (Bransford, Brown, and Cocking 2000; McNeill and Krajcik In press-b; also see Chapter 2 in this book) and our work with teachers, we have identified five different strategies teachers can use to support students in writing scientific explanations.

1. Make the framework explicit.

2. Model and critique explanations.

3. Provide a rationale for creating explanations.

4. Connect to everyday explanations.

5. Assess and provide feedback to students.

In the following section, these instructional strategies are described in more detail, along with examples from six teachers who enacted the Stuff unit.

## Strategy 1. Making the Framework Explicit

When discussing scientific explanations, teachers cannot assume that students understand how to create an explanation. Many of the teachers we work with explicitly discuss what an explanation is and define the different components of an explanation (claim, evidence, and reasoning) with their students. They discuss what the different components mean in science. Typically, they find that the claim is the easiest component for students to understand, while students have more difficulty with the concepts of evidence and reasoning. Teachers can have extensive conversations around the meanings of *evidence* and *reasoning* to help students understand these components, which can then translate into students more accurately including these components in their writing.

For example, when introducing scientific explanations to her students, one teacher, Ms. Nelson, asked her class what they thought evidence meant. The class initially came up with the definition "the data you have from actually doing something." The discussion continued with the class differentiating between data and evidence. They decided that not all data would count as good evidence and developed a more refined definition of evidence.

One student said, "You have to have more than one piece of evidence." This comment introduced the idea of providing sufficient evidence. Classroom conversation continued to include other characteristics of evidence, such as accuracy and appropriateness. Ms. Nelson summarized their discussion by saying, "So not only does the evidence have to be accurate and we have to have enough of it, but we also need to decide if the evidence is pertinent for our claim." As a class, the students developed a definition of evidence, including what counted as good evidence to support a claim (i.e., sufficiency, accuracy, and appropriateness).

Other teachers lead classrooms discussions on the concept of reasoning. Mr. Davis focused on how the reasoning, in his words, "ties the evidence back up to the original claim." Ms. Parker focused more on the idea that "reasoning is the scientific principle or justification for an answer." Discussing the reasoning helps students understand that they need to write explicitly in their explanations what underlying scientific principle they are using to select their evidence. Often students feel that the teacher already knows the scientific principle (like what a chemical reaction is or what biodiversity is), so they do not need to include it in their writing. Focusing on reasoning can help students include this justification.

# Strategy 2. Modeling and Critiquing Explanations

Besides defining scientific explanation, teachers also need to model and critique explanations for students. Teachers can provide models of explanations through either spoken examples or written examples. Teachers need to explicitly identify the strengths and weaknesses of those examples. Students can benefit from observing a strong example of reasoning that clearly includes a scientific principle to show why the evidence supports the claim. They cannot benefit from weak examples that need improvement, such as an example that uses both opinion and data as evidence. Weak examples can be used to highlight particular difficulties or misconceptions teachers may know that their students hold. Using these types of examples can help students understand how to write high-quality explanations in different content areas and how to be more critical of their own writing.

During one lesson of the Stuff unit, students write scientific explanations about whether fat and soap are the same or different substances. The curriculum materials suggest that teachers show the students examples of strong and weak explanations and model how to critique them. The following example is from Ms. Henry's classroom. After placing the written example on the overhead, she asked her students to critique it:

> *Fat and soap are both stuff, but they are different substances. Fat is used for cooking and soap is used for washing. They are both things we use everyday. The data table is my evidence that they are different substances. Stuff can be different substances if you have the right data to show it.*

The class agreed that this was a weak example of a scientific explanation. They then had the following conversation about the appropriateness of the evidence for the claim.

MS. HENRY:  Look at the second sentence—fat is used for cooking and soap is used for washing.

[Students laugh.]

MS. HENRY:  Who cares? Why does that matter? Because fat is used for cooking, is that what makes it fat?

STUDENTS:  No.

MS. HENRY:  No. OK. That does not mean anything to me. Is use— how something is used—is that a property?

STUDENTS:  No.

MS. HENRY:  No. Soap is used for washing. So what? That does not tell me if they are the same or different. Look at that

sentence there: "They are both things we use every day."
Thank you for the information, but that does not help
us at all. We use a lot of things every day. Next sentence.
Did they give us some good evidence?"

STUDENTS:     No.

MS. HENRY:     They say the data table is my evidence.

[Students laugh.]

MS. HENRY:     What about the data table? I don't know [gestures hands
in the air]. What on the data table? I don't know… you
did not give me any data to prove anything.

Although her class quickly agreed that the explanation was weak, Ms. Henry
took time to discuss the weaknesses of the evidence. She talked about how
use is not an appropriate piece of evidence because it is not a property. She
also indicated that just referring to the data table is not appropriate evidence.
She next showed a strong explanation, which included specific data about
density, melting point, and solubility to further model what is and is not
appropriate evidence for this claim. By modeling and critiquing examples,
she helped her students understand what is and is not a good example of a
scientific explanation.

# Strategy 3. Providing a Rationale for Creating Explanations

To effectively create scientific explanations, students should understand why
they need to engage in this inquiry practice. Otherwise, using the scientific explanation framework (i.e., claim, evidence, and reasoning) can become too procedural or algorithmic and students may not understand its value and purpose.

In our observations, we identified two different types of rationales for scientific explanation that teachers discuss with their students. Some teachers discuss
how science is fundamentally about explaining phenomena. For example,
Ms. Nelson discussed with her students that science is about explaining phenomena. She told her class, "Explaining is probably the most important part
of figuring out what is going on in science. It is what scientists do the most."
She often talked about how her students were scientists and that they engaged
in real science through inquiry such as explaining phenomena.

Another rationale teachers used for engaging in scientific explanation is that students need to be able to persuade others that their claims are justified. When writing an explanation, students tend to write a claim alone, without providing appropriate justification or support. Teachers can help students understand that providing evidence and reasoning creates a stronger case for the claim. For example, Mr. Kaplan held the following discussion with his class:

MR. KAPLAN:     If you are really trying to convince somebody of something, do you want to be as specific as possible?

STUDENT:        I wasn't convincing anybody.

MR. KAPLAN:     Well, that is what you want to convey. You want to convince someone of the claim. Your claim is that these two things are different substances. The evidence that you are using or choosing supports that.

Mr. Kaplan tried to help his students understand that the goal of the scientific explanation was to convince others of their claim. His students did not naturally understand this goal. Discussing the rationale behind an explanation can help students see the value and importance of the different components.

# Strategy 4. Connecting to Everyday Explanations

Just as in science, in everyday life people try to convince each other of claims. Discussing this similarity between science and everyday life may help students understand the purpose behind scientific explanation and build on their prior knowledge from their everyday experiences. Teachers can provide students with different everyday examples (like discussing who the best basketball player is or ways to convince your parents that you deserve a higher allowance) to discuss how the claim, evidence, and reasoning framework can be used. Drawing on what students know about evidence or justification in their everyday lives can help them understand those same concepts in science.

For example, Ms. Sutton placed the following example on the overhead as a journal topic when students entered the classroom.

**Evaluate the scientific explanation below:**

*The Temptations are the best band ever. They have a popular song and I like it. Therefore, they are the best band ever.*

Ms. Sutton then asked students how they evaluated the explanation, which resulted in the following conversation.

STUDENT 1: You did not have enough evidence to back it up.

Ms. SUTTON: Ah, so you are saying I can go around making this claim, but I don't have the kind of evidence that I would need?

STUDENT 1: Yes.

Ms. SUTTON: What, I have not convinced you with this?

STUDENTS: No.

Ms. SUTTON: This evidence is not good enough—they have a popular song and I like it?

STUDENTS: No.

Ms. SUTTON: What else is there? I like it.

STUDENT 1: It is your opinion.

Ms. SUTTON: Oh, it is my opinion. And that is not good for evidence?

STUDENTS: No.

Ms. SUTTON: But it is a fact that I like it.

STUDENT 1: It is not enough evidence.

Ms. SUTTON: What would be better evidence then?

STUDENT 1: Having a vote.

Ms. SUTTON: Ah. Having a vote, taking a survey. What if I asked 100 people, and 90 of them said that they like the Temptations?

STUDENT 1: Then that is enough evidence.

Ms. SUTTON: That is better evidence. Does anyone else have an idea of where I can get some good evidence to back up my claim? [Points to a student.]

STUDENT 2:      You did not include reasoning.

MS. SUTTON:     I do not have any kind of reasoning. I have no logical
                reason why I said that. I just throw it out there that they
                have a popular song and I like that and I hope that you
                accept it. I need some reasoning—some kind off logic
                to back that up.

The class continued to discuss what would count as good evidence and good
reasoning. They decided that good reasoning includes a general principle
about why a band could be considered the best band ever. Specifically, they
decided the reasoning should be, "In order to be the best band, you must have
millions of fans and sell millions of records." Then they determined that their
evidence would be, "The Temptations fan club has one million members,"
and "They earned four gold records." Ms. Sutton used this opportunity to
discuss the difference between evidence and opinion and to stress the importance of using logic to support why your evidence supports your claim. She
used this everyday example to help students understand the claim, evidence,
and reasoning framework, as well as the idea that students are trying to persuade or convince someone of their claim.

Although scientific explanations have similar features as everyday explanations, the two types of explanation can also differ substantially. Besides talking about similarities with everyday examples, it can also be important to
talk about differences. When people use the word *explain* in everyday talk,
they are often not asking for someone to provide evidence and reasoning
for a claim. For example, someone might ask you, "Can you explain to me
where the grocery store is?" In this case, the meaning of *explain* corresponds
more closely to *describe* than to the scientific explanation framework of claim,
evidence, and reasoning. Students can develop a more complete understanding of scientific explanation if they understand how it is similar and different
from everyday explanations.

# Strategy 5. Assessing and Providing Feedback to Students

When students write scientific explanations, their thinking may become
more visible, both in terms of their understanding of the science content and
their reasoning about data. We developed a base explanation rubric to help
teachers assess their students' understanding as revealed in their writing. This
is a general rubric for scoring scientific explanations across different content

and learning tasks (see Appendix B, p. 134). It includes the three components of a scientific explanation and offers guidance for thinking about different levels of student achievement for each of those components. Teachers adapt the base rubric for a particular task by taking into consideration the content knowledge needed to respond to the task as well as considering what counts as appropriate evidence and reasoning.

When assessing students' explanations, teachers need to provide explicit and thorough feedback. Telling students only that their explanation is "good" or "weak" does not necessarily provide them with any guidance on how to improve. Teachers can provide specific feedback on a variety of different aspects, such as the components of the explanation (i.e., claim, evidence, and reasoning), the science content of the explanation, and the holistic quality of the explanation. In providing feedback, teachers need to point out strengths and weaknesses. For example, Mr. Kaplan circulated around the room and provided students with feedback, often pointing out the strengths and weaknesses of students' explanations—for example, "Your claim said they were different. You need some evidence to show that."

Another effective feedback strategy is offering suggestions on how to improve. Mr. Kaplan provided one student with suggestions on how to improve his evidence as follows: "Now, you have to be more specific—the color changed from this to this; this changed from this to this…. Be as specific as possible." A third feedback strategy is to ask questions that promote deeper thinking. For example, in order to encourage one student to revise her reasoning, Mr. Kaplan asked her, "What scientific principle explains this?" Using these different feedback strategies can help students revise their current scientific explanations, as well develop a deeper understanding of both the content and how to write an explanation.

# Conclusion

Constructing scientific explanations in which students support their claims with appropriate evidence and reasoning is an important element of scientific inquiry (AAAS 1993; NRC 1996). Engaging in explanation can help students develop a deeper understanding of the science content and become more adept at writing and critiquing explanations. Yet this complex inquiry practice is rarely a part of classroom instruction, and students often have difficulty supporting their scientific claims (Sadler 2004).

The role of teachers and the different instructional strategies they incorporate into their classroom instruction is important for students' success at writing explanations and building students' understanding of the content. Using the strategies discussed in this chapter can help make scientific explanation an essential and successful part of classroom inquiry. Furthermore, as students become more successful at writing scientific explanations, teachers can introduce more complex tasks. Students can analyze data from phenomena where there are multiple possible explanations (see Chapters 4 and 8). Students can rule out alternative explanations by showing that there is not enough evidence to support a claim or there is counterevidence for a claim. After analyzing the data and constructing their explanations, they can debate the strength of their explanations. These tasks are important for helping students become scientifically literate where they critically evaluate scientific claims presented in popular culture (e.g., newspapers and magazines).

Although we have focused on written explanations, these strategies can also encourage scientific talk in the classroom where evidence and reasoning are valued. The goal is to help students become critical thinkers and successfully engage in scientific inquiry to explain phenomena.

## Acknowledgments

This research referred to in this chapter was supported in part by the National Science Foundation grants ESI 0101780 and ESI 0227557. Any opinions expressed in this work are those of the authors and do not necessarily represent those of the funding agency or the University of Michigan.

# Appendix A:
# Substance and Property Explanation

Examine the following data table:

|  | Density | Color | Mass | Melting Point |
|---|---|---|---|---|
| Liquid 1 | 0.93 g/cm³ | no color | 38 g | -98 °C |
| Liquid 2 | 0.79 g/cm³ | no color | 38 g | 26 °C |
| Liquid 3 | 13.6 g/cm³ | silver | 21 g | -39 °C |
| Liquid 4 | 0.93 g/cm³ | no color | 16 g | -98 °C |

Write a **scientific explanation** that states whether any of the liquids are the same substance.

# Appendix B: Base Explanation Rubric

| Component | Level | | |
|---|---|---|---|
| | 0 | 1 | 2 |
| *Claim*—A conclusion that answers the original question. | Does not make a claim, or makes an inaccurate claim. | Makes an accurate but incomplete claim. | Makes an accurate and complete claim. |
| *Evidence*—Scientific data that supports the claim. The data needs to be appropriate and sufficient to support the claim. | Does not provide evidence, or only provides inappropriate evidence (evidence that does not support claim). | Provides appropriate but insufficient evidence to support claim. May include some inappropriate evidence. | Provides appropriate and sufficient evidence to support claim. |
| *Reasoning*—A justification that links the claim and evidence. It shows why the data count as evidence by using appropriate and sufficient scientific principles. | Does not provide reasoning, or only provides reasoning that does not link evidence to claim. | Provides reasoning that links the claim and evidence. Repeats the evidence and/or includes some—but not sufficient—scientific principles. | Provides reasoning that links evidence to claim. Includes appropriate and sufficient scientific principles. |

# References

Aarons, A. B. 1990. *A guide to introductory physics teaching*. New York: John Wiley and Sons.

American Association for the Advancement of Science (AAAS). 1990. *Science for all Americans*. New York: Oxford University Press.

American Association for the Advancement of Science (AAAS). 1993. *Benchmarks for science literacy*. New York: Oxford University Press.

Ault, C. R., Jr. 1998. Criteria of excellence for geological inquiry: The necessity of ambiguity. *Journal of Research in Science Teaching* 35(2): 189–212.

Ausubel, D. P. 1963. *The psychology of meaningful verbal learning*. New York: Grune and Stratton.

Barman, C. R., and J. D. Stockton. 2002. An evaluation of the SOAR–High Project: A web-based science program for deaf students. *American Annals of the Deaf* 147(3): 5–10.

Bay, M., J. R. Staver, T. Bryan, and J. Hale.1992. Science instruction for the mildly handicapped: Direct instruction versus discovery teaching. *Journal of Research in Science Teaching* 29(6): 555–570.

Bell, P. 2005. *The school science laboratory: Considerations of learning, technology and scientific practice*. Washington, DC: National Academies Press.

Bell, P., and M. Linn. 2000. Scientific arguments as learning artifacts: Designing for learning from the web with KIE. *International Journal of Science Education* 22(8): 797–817.

Biological Sciences Curriculum Study (BSCS). 1994. *BSCS middle school science and technology, teacher's guide.* Dubuque, IA: Kendall Hunt.

Bishop, B. 1985. The social construction of meaning—A significant development in mathematics education. *For the Learning of Mathematics* 5: 24–28.

Borron, R. 1978. Modifying science instruction to meet the needs of the hearing impaired. *Journal of Research in Science Teaching* 15(4): 257–262.

Bransford, J. D., A. L. Brown, and R. R. Cocking, eds. 2000. *How people learn: Brain, mind, experience, and school.* Washington, DC: National Academy Press.

Bruner, J. 1961. The act of discovery. *Harvard Educational Review* 31: 21.

Burgstahler, S. 2004. *Universal design of instruction.* Retrieved January 12, 2007, from the University of Washington DO-IT website: *www.washington.edu/doit/Stem/ud.html*

Bybee, R. W. 1977. Toward a third century in science education. *The American Biology Teacher* 39(6): 338.

Bybee, R. W. 1997. *Achieving scientific literacy.* Portsmouth, NH: Heinemann.

Caldwell, O. W. 1920. *Reorganization of science in secondary schools* (Bulletin No. 26). Washington, DC: Commission on Reorganization of Secondary Education, Bureau of Education, U.S. Department of the Interior.

Caldwell, O. W. 1924. Report of the American Association for the Advancement of Science, Committee on the Place of Science in Education. *Science* 60: 534.

Carnap, R. 1995. *An introduction to the philosophy of science.* New York: Dover.

Cartier, J. 2000. *Using a modeling approach to explore scientific epistemology with high school biology students* (Research Report No. 99–1). Retrieved January 25, 2007, from the Wisconsin Center for Educational Research web site: *www.wcer.wisc.edu/ncisla/publications/reports/RR99–1.pdf*

Cawley, J, and R. Parmar. 2001. Literacy proficiency and science for students with learning disabilities. *Reading and Writing Quarterly* 17: 105–125.

Central Association of Science and Mathematics Teachers. 1915. Report of the Central Association of Science and Mathematics Teachers Committee on the Unified High School Science Course. *School Science and Mathematics* 15(4): 334.

Chinn, C., and B. Malhotra. 2002. Epistemologically authentic inquiry in schools: A theoretical framework for evaluating inquiry tasks. *Science Education* 86: 175–218.

Collette, A. T., and E. L. Chiappetta. 1989. *Science instruction in the middle and secondary schools.* Columbus, OH: Merrill.

Commission on the Reorganization of Secondary Education. 1918. *The cardinal principles of secondary education* (Bulletin No. 35). Washington, DC: U.S. Office of Education, U.S. Government Printing Office.

Committee on Secondary School Studies. 1893. *Report of the Committee of Ten on secondary school studies.* Washington, DC: National Education Association.

Dalton, B., C. Morocco, T. Tivnan, and P. Mead. 1997. Supported inquiry science: Teaching for conceptual change in urban and suburban science classrooms. *Journal of Learning Disabilities* 30(6): 670–684.

DeBoer, G. E. 2000. *A history of ideas in science education: Implications for practice.* New York: Teachers College, Columbia University.

Dewey, J. 1910. *How we think.* Mineola, NY: Dover.

Dewey, J. 1938. *Experience and education.* New York: Macmillan.

Donohoe, K., and M. Zigmond. 1988. High school grades of urban LD students and low achieving peers. Paper presented at the annual meeting of the American Educational Research Association, San Francisco, CA (April).

Donovan, M. S., and J. D. Bransford. 2005. *How students learn: Science in the classroom.* Washington DC: National Academies Press.

Driver, R., and B. F. Bell. 1986. Students' thinking and the learning of science: A constructivist view. *School Science Review* 67: 443–456.

Driver, R., and J. Easley. 1978. Pupils and paradigms: A review of literature related to concept development in adolescent science students. *Studies in Science Education* 5: 61–84.

Driver, R., J. Leach, R. Millar, and P. Scott. 1996. *Young people's images of science.* Buckingham, UK: Open University Press.

Driver, R., P. Newton, and J. Osborne. 2000. Establishing the norms of scientific argumentation in classrooms. *Science Education* 84(3): 287–312.

Erwin, E., J. Ayala, and T. Perkins. 2001. You don't have to be sighted to be a scientist do you? Issues and outcomes in science education. *Journal of Visual Impairment and Blindness* 95: 338–352.

Ford, D. 2006. Representation of science within children's trade books. *Journal of Research in Science Teaching* 43: 214–235.

Frank, J., G. R. Luera, and W. B. Stapp. 1996. *Air pollution ozone study and action.* Dubuque, IA: Kendall/Hunt.

Giere, R. N. 1991. *Understanding scientific reasoning* (3rd ed.). New York: Harcourt Brace Jovanovich.

Glickstein, N. 2002. Seeing isn't always believing: Investigating the reliability of science demonstrations. *The Science Teacher* 69: 41–43.

Hake, R. 1992. Socratic pedagogy in the introductory physics laboratory. *The Physics Teacher* 30(9): 546–552.

Harms, N. C., and R. E. Yager, eds. 1981. *What research says to the science teacher* (Vol. 3). Washington, DC: National Science Teachers Association.

Harnisch, D., and I. Wilkinson. 1989. Cognitive return of schooling for the handicapped: Preliminary findings from high school and beyond. Paper presented at the annual meeting of the American Educational Research Association, San Francisco, CA.

Hodson, D. 1991. Philosophy of science and science education. In *History, philosophy, and science teaching: Selected readings,* ed. M. R. Matthews, 19–32. Toronto: OISE Press.

Howe, Q. 1991. *Under running laughter: Notes from a renegade classroom.* New York: Macmillan.

Jiménez–Aleixandre, M. P., A. B. Rodríguez, and R. A. Duschl. 2000. "Doing the lesson" or "doing science": Argument in high school genetics. *Science Education* 84: 757–792.

Kuhn, D. 1993. Science as argument: Implications for teaching and learning scientific thinking. *Science Education* 77: 319–338.

Lampkin, R. H. 1951. Scientific inquiry for science teachers. *Science Education* 35: 17–39.

Lerman, S. 1989. Constructivism, mathematics, and mathematics education. *Educational Studies of Mathematics* 20: 211–223.

Longino, H. 1990. *Science as social knowledge: Values and objectivity in scientific inquiry.* Princeton, NJ: Princeton University Press.

Louisell, W. H. 1973. *Quantum statistical properties of radiation.* New York: Wiley.

Magnussen, S., and A. Palincsar. 2005. Teaching to promote the development of scientific knowledge and reasoning about light at the elementary school level. In *How students learn history, mathematics, and science in the classroom,* eds. M. Donovan and J. Bransford, 421–459. Washington, DC: National Academies Press.

Mastropieri, M., and T. Scruggs. 1992. Science for students with disabilities. *Review of Educational Research* 62(4): 377–411.

Mastropieri, M., T. Scruggs, R. Boon, and K. Butcher. 2001. Correlations of inquiry learning in science. *Remedial and Special Education* 22(3): 130–137.

McNeill, K. L., C. J. Harris, M. Heitzman, D. J. Lizotte, L. M. Sutherland, and J. Krajcik. 2004. How can I make new stuff from old stuff? In *IQWST: Investigating and questioning our world through science and technology*, eds. J. Krajcik and B. J. Reiser. Ann Arbor, MI: University of Michigan.

McNeill, K. L., and J. Krajcik. In press (a). Middle school students' use of appropriate and inappropriate evidence in writing scientific explanations. In *Thinking with data: The proceedings of the 33rd Carnegie Symposium on Cognition*, eds. M. Lovett and P. Shah. Mahwah, NJ: Lawrence Erlbaum.

McNeill, K. L. and J. Krajcik. In press (b). Scientific explanations: Characterizing and evaluating the effects of teachers' instructional practices on student learning. *Journal of Research in Science Teaching.*

McNeill, K. L., D. J. Lizotte, J. Krajcik, and R. W. Marx. 2006. Supporting students' construction of scientific explanations by fading scaffolds in instructional materials. *The Journal of the Learning Sciences* 15(2): 153–191.

Millar, R. 2004. *The role of practical work in the teaching and learning of science.* Washington, DC: National Academies Press.

Minstrell, J., and E. H. van Zee, eds. 2000. *Inquiring into inquiry learning and teaching in science.* Washington, DC: American Association for the Advancement of Science.

Moje, E. B., D. Peek-Brown, L. M. Sutherland, R. W. Marx, P. Blumenfeld, and J. Krajcik. 2004. Explaining explanations: Developing scientific literacy in middle-school project-based science reforms. In *Bridging the gap: Improving literacy learning for preadolescent and adolescent learners in grades 4–12*, eds. D. Strickland and D. E. Alvermann. New York: Teachers College Press.

Monk, M., and J. Dillon, eds. 1995. *Learning to teach science: Activities for student teachers and mentors.* London: Falmer.

National Center for Education Statistics. 2003. *Children 3 to 21 years old served in federally supported programs for the disabled, by type of disability: Selected years, 1976–77 to 2001–02.* Washington, DC: Author.

National Commission on Excellence in Education. 1983. *A nation at risk: The imperative for education reform* (Report No. 065–000–001772). Washington, DC: U.S. Government Printing Office.

National Research Council (NRC). 1996. *National science education standards.* Washington, DC: National Academy Press.

National Research Council (NRC). 2000. *Inquiry and the national science education standards.* Washington, DC: National Academy Press.

Newton, P., R. Driver, and J. Osborne. 1999. The place of argumentation in the pedagogy of school science. *International Journal of Science Education* 21(5): 553–576.

Nisbett, R. E., and L. Ross. 1980. *Human inference: Strategies and shortcomings of social judgment.* Englewood Cliffs, NJ: Prentice–Hall.

Norris, S.P., and L. M. Phillips. 2003. How literacy in its fundamental sense is central to scientific literacy. *Science Education* 87: 224–240.

Novak, J. 1990. Concept maps and Vee diagrams: Two metacognitive tools to facilitate meaningful learning. *Instructional Scienc*e 19(1): 29–52.

Null, R. L. 1996. *Universal design: Creative solutions for ADA compliance.* Belmont, CA: Professional Publications.

Odubunmi, O., and T. A. Balogun. 1991. The effect of laboratory and lecture teaching methods on cognitive achievement in integrated science. *Journal of Research in Science Teaching* 28(3): 213–224.

Palincsar, A. S., S. J. Magnusson, K. M. Collins, and J. Cutter. 2001. Making science accessible to all: Results of a design experiment in inclusive classrooms. *Learning Disability Quarterly* 24(1): 15–32.

Piaget, J. 1970. *Genetic epistemology.* New York: Columbia University Press.

Pinkerton, K. D. 1998. Network similarity (NETSIM) as a method of assessing structural knowledge for large groups. *Journal of Interactive Learning Research* 9(3/4): 249–270.

Pinkerton, K. D. 2005. Learning from mistakes. *The Physics Teacher* 43(8): 510–513.

Progressive Education Association. 1938. *Science in general education.* New York: Appleton-Century Crofts.

Reddy, M. 1979. The conduit metaphor. In *Metaphor and thought,* ed. A. Ortony, 284–297. New York: Cambridge University Press.

Richardson, V. 2000. Searching for a center. *Teaching and Teacher Education* 16: 905–909.

Rogoff, B. 1990. *Apprenticeship in thinking: Cognitive development in social context.* Oxford, England: Oxford University Press.

Rose, D. H., and A. Meyer. 2002. *Teaching every student in the digital age: Universal design for learning.* Alexandria, VA: Association for Supervision and Curriculum Development.

Sadler, T. D. 2004. Informal reasoning regarding socioscientific issues: A critical review of research. *Journal of Research in Science Teaching* 41(5): 513–536.

Sandoval, W. A., and B. Reiser. 2003. Explanation-driven inquiry: Integrating conceptual and epistemic scaffolds for scientific inquiry. *Science Education* 88(3): 345–372.

Schwab, J. 1962. The teaching of science as enquiry. In *The teaching of science,* eds. J. Schwab and P. Brandwein, 3–10. Cambridge, MA: Harvard University Press.

Schwarz, C., and B. White. 2005. Metamodeling knowledge: Developing students' understanding of scientific modeling. *Cognition and Instruction* 23(2): 165–205.

Scruggs, T., M. Mastropieri, and R. Boon. 1998. Science education for students with disabilities: A review of recent research. *Studies in Science Education* 32: 21–44.

Stevens, A. L., and A. Collins. 1980. Multiple conceptual models of a complex system. In *Aptitude learning and instruction. Volume 2: Cognitive process analysis of learning in problem solving,* eds. R. E. Snow, P. A. Federico, and W. E. Montague. Hillsdale, NJ: Lawrence Earlbaum.

Stapp, W. B., A. Wols, and S. L. Staukoub. 1996. *Environmental education for empowerment: Action research and community problem solving.* Dubuque, IA: Kendall/Hunt.

Toulmin, S. 1958. *The uses of argument.* Cambridge, UK: Cambridge University Press.

University of Washington. 1999. *Working together: Science teachers and students with disabilities.* Washington, DC: Department of Education. (ERIC Document Reproduction Service No. ED 481 294)

Vygotsky, L. S. (trans. by A. Kozulin). 1962/1986. *Thought and language.* Cambridge, MA: MIT Press.

Wells, M., D. Hestenes, and G. Swackhamer. 1995. A modeling method for high school physics. *American Journal of Physics* 63(7): 606–619.

Westbury, I., and N. J. Wilkof, eds. 1978. *Joseph Schwab: Science, curriculum, and liberal education.* Chicago: The University of Chicago Press.

Wiggins, G., and J. McTighe. 2005. *Understanding by design* (2nd ed.). Alexandria, VA: Association for Supervision and Curriculum Development.

Zohar, A., and F. Nemet. 2002. Fostering students' knowledge and argumentation skills through dilemmas in human genetics. *Journal of Research in Science Teaching* 39(1): 35–62.

# Editors

**Julie Luft** is a professor of science education at the Mary Lou Fulton College of Education at Arizona State University–Tempe.

**Randy L. Bell** is an associate professor at the Curry School of Education at the University of Virginia.

**Julie Gess-Newsome** is the J. Lawrence Walkup Distinguished Professor of Science Education in the Department of Teaching and Learning at Northern Arizona University.

# Contributors

**S. Raj Chaudhury** is an associate professor in the Department of Physics, Computer Science, and Engineering at Christopher Newport University.

**Eugene L. Chiappetta** is a professor in the Department of Curriculum and Instruction at the University of Houston.

**Douglas B. Clark** is an assistant professor in the Department of Curriculum and Instruction at Arizona State University–Tempe.

**Brett Criswell** was a chemistry teacher at Central Columbia High School, Bloomsburg, Pennsylvania, at the time his article was written. He is now a PhD student at Pennsylvania State University.

**Oliver Dreon, Jr.,** is a physics teacher at Cumberland Valley High School, Mechanicsburg, Pennsylvania.

**Joseph Krajcik** is a professor of science education in the School of Education at the University of Michigan.

**Theodore J. Leuenberger** is a science teacher at Benton Central Jr./Sr. High School, Oxford, Indiana.

**Scott McDonald** is an assistant professor of science education in the Department of Curriculum and Instruction at Pennsylvania State University.

**Katherine L. McNeill** is an assistant professor of science education in the Lynch School of Education, Boston College.

**Catherine Milne** is an assistant professor of science education in the Steinhardt School of Culture, Education, and Human Development at New York University.

**Stephen P. Norris** is a professor and the Canada Research Chair in the Department of Educational Policy Studies at the University of Alberta, Edmonton.

**Jonathan F. Osborne** is a professor of science education in the Department of Education and Professional Studies at King's College, London.

**Linda M. Phillips** is a professor and the director of the Canadian Centre for Research on Literacy at the University of Alberta, Edmonton.

**K. David Pinkerton** is a science educator at the BSCS Center for Curriculum Development at BSCS (Biological Sciences Curriculum Study), Colorado Springs, Colorado.

**Eric J. Pyle** is an associate professor in the Department of Geology and Environmental Sciences at James Madison University.

**Daniel P. Shepardson** is a professor of geoenvironmental and science education in the Department of Curriculum and Instruction at Purdue University.

**Kathy Cabe Trundle** is an assistant professor in the School of Teaching and Learning at Ohio State University.

**Pamela Van Scotter** is the director of the BSCS Center for Curriculum Development at BSCS (Biological Sciences Curriculum Study), Colorado Springs, Colorado.

**Mark Windschitl** is an associate professor of science education in the College of Education at the University of Washington.

# Index

*Page numbers in **boldface** type refer to figures or tables.*